PRAISE FOR
THE PEACE CORPS VOLUNTEER'S HANDBOOK

"The *Peace Corps Volunteer's Handbook* is a fantastic companion for any applicant on their journey to becoming a PCV. As a campus recruiter, I am constantly interacting with potential applicants who want to know as much as possible about Peace Corps. This book will enhance my advice and guidance when working with them. It is entertaining to read and REAL—no matter how unique each experience is, it all boils down to what is in this book. I love that it is YOURS and can help in YOUR journey as a PCV. To make it even better, you can give this and the experiences you write in this book to help future Volunteers. It's a must read! Enjoy the accomplishments, challenges, growth, friendships, embarrassing moments, and laughter that you have while in Peace Corps. And don't forget to pay it forward!"

—Amy Panikowski, RPCV (Malawi 00-01), University of Florida Peace Corps Recruiter (05-10)

"Travis' book is an invaluable resource for those thinking about applying to Peace Corps, those currently serving, and even those who have returned after their service. Based on his own personal experience, and those of other volunteers and applicants, he goes through the process step by step, explaining the application process, the ups and downs of living in a developing country, and how to make the most of your service!"

—Mike Sheppard, RPCV (The Gambia 03-05),
Founder of *PeaceCorpsWiki.org* and
PeaceCorpsJournals.com

"You lucky *@^%!?#$ don't know how lucky you are to have such a kickass handbook written for you. This handbook is full of helpful suggestions and wisdom for a wide variety of PC experiences, even the apocalyptic ones. Now, at the end of my service, I still find myself going back to this book for advice on reviving my enthusiasm for the 'toughest job I'll ever love,' keeping my 'American standards' in check, and just being a good Volunteer in general.

Luggage space is precious when one travels, but this handbook will definitely be in my backpack home. It's not simply a reminder of all the lessons I've learned from my PC experience but a personal scrapbook that is uniquely mine. Plus, what else is going to stop me from hyperventilating whenever I go into culture shock? Be grateful…"

—Alexandra Yang, RPCV (Mongolia 08-10)

"Lucky you! Peace Corps Volunteer service is not just an opportunity; it's an AMAZING opportunity—and a privilege. You join a 50-year legacy of Americans who make a difference in communities overseas, and then continue to change the world long after their service is complete. By addressing not just the practicalities of the Peace Corps, but the emotional and psychological aspects, *The Peace Corps Volunteer's Handbook* provides invaluable, down-to-earth advice that can help you make the most of this transformative experience, as well as guide you when you come home."

—Erica Burman, RPCV (The Gambia 87-89),
Director of Communications and Editor of
Worldview Magazine, National Peace Corps
Association

"I have found that *The Peace Corps Volunteer's Handbook* contains the most extensive explanation of the application process available. Honest testimonials from current and returned Peace Corps Volunteers serve as the most valuable resource, and the handbook is full of relevant information and insight. Currently nominated for an assignment in Eastern Europe, I would like to thank the contributors to the handbook for aiding in making my application process as smooth as possible. The handbook will surely continue to be a valuable resource for me while I serve and a recommended read for all those interested in the Peace Corps."

—Julie Nelson, Peace Corps Nominee (10-12)

"The must-have book for anyone thinking of joining the Peace Corps (as well as current Volunteers). Not only is *The Peace Corps Volunteer's Handbook* filled with insight into what it's like to be a PCV, the book becomes your own personal keepsake with interactive sections and chapters; something to reflect upon long after you've returned home. Every PCV's experience is unique, but this book succeeds in weaving the Peace Corps Experience into an invaluable resource for before, during, and after your service."

—Christopher Beale, RPCV (Eastern Caribbean
05-07), Founder of *Other Places Travel Guides
by RPCVs*

"Being a Peace Corps Volunteer is a wonderful experience, but it's also not right for everyone. The tips and candid information in *The Peace Corps Volunteer's Handbook* will be a great tool for helping you decide if Peace Corps might be right for you."

—Jim Carl, RPCV (Swaziland 79-81),
Country Director (Mongolia 07-10)

"*The Peace Corps Volunteer's Handbook* is a great tool to learn more about the Peace Corps from the inside. The RPCV in me wishes something like this would have been available when I was deciding what the next step in my post-university life should be. The former Peace Corps recruiter and placement officer in me wants to remind you that each applicant's experience is unique and nothing you read anywhere will be exactly how it will be for you. Therefore please use this book just for what it is...a tool to teach you more about how absolutely life-changing the Peace Corps can be. Use the tips to help navigate your way through the long application process. But above all else, use this book as inspiration, not as gospel. Peace Corps policies, trainings, programs, even the countries we serve in will change over time. Be flexible and you will be a Peace Corps Volunteer one day!"

—Jason Bowers, RPCV (Slovak Republic 00-02),
Peace Corps Recruiter & Placement Officer (04-10)

THE

PEACE CORPS VOLUNTEER'S HANDBOOK

A Personal Field Guide to Making
the Most of Your
Peace Corps Experience

TRAVIS HELLSTROM

Foreword by Kevin F. F. Quigley, Ph.D.
Former President of the
National Peace Corps Association

hatherleigh
Improve your life. Change your world.

hatherleigh
e your life. Change your world.

Hatherleigh Press is committed to preserving and protecting the natural
resources of the earth. Environmentally responsible and sustainable
practices are embraced within the company's mission statement.

Visit us at www.hatherleighpress.com and register online for free offers, discounts,
special events, and more.

Library of Congress Cataloging-in-Publication Data is available upon request.
ISBN 978-1-57826-645-6

All Hatherleigh Press titles are available for bulk purchase, special promotions, and
premiums. For information about reselling and special purchase opportunities, please call
1-800-528-2550 and ask for the Special Sales Manager.

Cover and Interior Design by Cynthia Dunne

10 9 8 7 6 5 4 3 2 1
Printed in the United States

TABLE OF CONTENTS

To those who are changing themselves
and changing the world.

THIS HANDBOOK WAS WRITTEN to benefit Peace Corps Volunteers and complement the existing resources and information available to help all Volunteers enjoy happy, healthy, and meaningful years of service. Please note that while we love the Peace Corps, we do not officially represent its opinions or those of the United States government. To learn more about the Peace Corps officially, please visit peacecorps.gov.

A portion of the proceeds from *The Peace Corps Volunteer's Handbook* goes to fund Peace Corps projects around the world. We achieve this through the Peace Corps Partnership Program, which is connected with Volunteers on the ground right now, making a difference in the lives of their community friends every day.

Peace Corps parade celebrating 50 years of Peace Corps (2011).

Students with a map from the Peace Corps World Map Project (2008).

FOREWORD

SINCE THE PEACE CORPS's launch more than a half-century
ago as perhaps one of the boldest experiments in how the United
States engages the world, its success has been built one story at a
time by the nearly quarter of a million individuals who, like me, are
privileged to have served as Volunteers.

Our accomplishments come not simply from the relationships
we develop with our counterparts, host families, and community
members, but most importantly, from the manner in which those
relationships are developed and nurtured. Wherever you serve,
whenever you serve, this involves approaching the communities we
serve on *their* terms, and continually trying to be empathetic learners motivated to make a difference in advancing your adopted community's dreams in ways big and small.

Don't be mistaken—this is really hard. This explains why Volunteers most often describe their service as "the toughest job you will
ever love." This is more than just a marketing slogan; it's actually
the best approximation of the myriad complexities, challenges, and
rewards of the Volunteer experience.

This remarkable *Peace Corps Volunteer's Handbook* provides many
helpful suggestions and points to invaluable resources that will help
you make your Peace Corps experience the most it can be. This
handbook ingeniously supplements the world-class training that the
Peace Corps provides in language-learning, working across cultures,
and applying your skills and experience in a new context.

Travis Hellstrom, along with an inspired team of dozens of current and former Volunteers, has done a great service in putting together this book. This effort grew out of their keen motivation to
ensure that their personal volunteer service had the greatest possible
impact. Doing that, they realized that their work in identifying best
practices and useful resources had much broader applications.

I first learned of Travis when he was serving as a Volunteer in Mongolia, where he was making remarkable use of communication technologies to deepen and broaden his work with local health and civic organizations. He provided invaluable perspectives to the National Peace Corps Association as one of the first members of a Serving Volunteer Advisory Council. This pioneering group strengthened NPCA's work in advancing the goals and values of the Peace Corps, and developed new strategies for supporting current and former Volunteers. My NPCA colleagues and I learned countless lessons from Travis and his collaborators. I am very pleased that Travis is building on his passion for learning and making a difference by currently serving as Chair of Marlboro College's Master's program for professionals in mission-driven organizations.

The experience of the 220,000+ Volunteers tells us that we get far more than we give. One of the most important things that we get is the all-too-rare chance to cultivate the practice of being life-long learners committed to serving our communities, wherever we find them. The evidence is clear that once a Volunteer, we are always a Volunteer.

With the help of *The Peace Corps Volunteer's Handbook*, you have practical advice and proven information and resources that will let you respond to our inspiring founder Sargent Shriver's exhortation of, "Serve, serve, serve." This book will help you do that in your Peace Corps community and in other communities after your Volunteer experience. This is the best way that we can all make progress in realizing the Peace Corps's vision of a more peaceful and prosperous world.

Kevin F. F. Quigley, Ph.D.

RETURNED PEACE CORPS VOLUNTEER (THAILAND 1976-79)
PRESIDENT, NATIONAL PEACE CORPS ASSOCIATION (2003-12)
COUNTRY DIRECTOR, PEACE CORPS THAILAND (2012-15)
PRESIDENT, MARLBORO COLLEGE (2015-PRESENT)

ACKNOWLEDGEMENTS

THEY SAY THAT IF you stand on the shoulders of giants you can see farther. That is the idea behind this handbook, as well as the way it was written. Here are some of our giants, those great friends and Volunteers who came together to help us all see a little farther.

Thank you to Donna Waldron, John Creech, and Taylor McCauley for your early support of this idea, which started years ago as a Peace Corps application guide for students at Campbell University.

Thank you to our many Peace Corps Volunteer friends who added their incredible ideas to this book, including Jeff Kuhn, Mary Manouchehri, Mike Prelaske, Dylan Bosch, Mike Sheppard, Ben Wiechman, James Kwon, Julie Nelson, Karlie Love, Liz Fuller, and Scott Wallick.

Thank you to Tunga Jargalsaihan, Alex Yang, Mark Rosenwald, Amy Lee, Alex Lyddon, Elaine Law, and Leslie Chamberlain for your encouragement and support throughout the creative process.

Thank you especially to our consultants, editors, and design team—Anna Hoyle, Todd Waite, Judy Gates, Claire Riley, Jason Bowers, Amy Panikowski, Chess Hoyle, Wee Wan, and Erica Burman—for your great efforts to successfully launch the first edition of this handbook.

Because of your hard work, our dream of helping Volunteers have happier, healthier, and more meaningful years of service can come true, while also raising money for Peace Corps projects along the way. Thank you from the bottom of my heart.

"Peace Corps JFK's Bold Legacy"
by Norman Rockwell (1966).

PREFACE

WHAT YOU HOLD IN your hands is designed to be a handbook for your Peace Corps adventure, no matter where you are in the process. As your pen touches this paper, you are already helping us write the next book. Any Volunteer can contribute to this handbook at any time and we couldn't be more excited to hear about your experiences.

We have designed this book so you can hold it in your hands, write in it as a journal of your experiences, and then share those experiences with future generations of Peace Corps Volunteers. In this way, others can learn from your experiences, add to them, and in turn give back to their Peace Corps communities. Every blank space was planned out for you to scribble your name on the front cover, doodle in the margins, improve on our methods, and share your own experiences so that someone else can learn from you, too. *The Peace Corps Volunteer's Handbook* is meant to be held in one hand with a pen in the other, ready to be made your own.

Thank you for letting us be here with you as you experience your Peace Corps adventure. We are excited to provide this resource so that we can continue making the Peace Corps an even more incredible experience for each and every Volunteer. Together, we can improve the Peace Corps community one book at a time—but only with your help. To join the conversation, visit travishellstrom.com/handbook. Thanks!

John F. Kennedy giving his famous 2 AM speech, first mentioning the idea of The Peace Corps at the University of Michigan (1960).

John F. Kennedy greeting the first Peace Corps Volunteers (1961).

INTRODUCTION

P EACE CORPS MAY JUST be 'the toughest job you'll ever love,' but you don't have to learn that the hard way. *The Peace Corps Volunteer's Handbook* is the handbook we wish someone would have given us: a collection of lessons learned from Volunteers all around the world, created to act as a companion on your adventure of applying to and serving in the Peace Corps. We hope you find what we've shared helpful. If not, don't worry—everyone's Peace Corps service is unique and we just hope you have an incredible experience. If at any time you have questions unanswered by this guide, please contact Peace Corps directly. Or, if you think we can help, please contact us through the Peace Corps Handbook website at travishellstrom.com/handbook.

About Peace Corps

Peace Corps is a United States governmental organization which celebrated its 55th anniversary in 2016. It was founded by President John F. Kennedy with the Peace Corps Act of March 1961. As an organization, the Peace Corps selects, assigns, and sponsors Volunteers to complete 27-month service assignments around the world and further the Peace Corps' mission "to promote world peace and friendship" through three goals:

- To help the people of interested countries in meeting their needs for trained men and women.
- To help promote a better understanding of Americans on the part of the peoples served.
- To help promote a better understanding of other peoples on the part of all Americans.

These three founding goals of Peace Corps were set down by Kennedy himself in 1961 and to this day, they remain the ideals of every Peace Corps Volunteer.

In general, the assignments of Peace Corps Volunteers are broken down into the areas of Education, Business & Information Technology, Health, Agriculture, and Community/Youth Development. However, hundreds of different assignments are given out every year in countries throughout the world. To say that every Peace Corps Volunteer has his or her own unique experience really is an understatement. Just as no Peace Corps Volunteer is the same as any other, no Peace Corps *job* is like any other. As hundreds of thousands of Volunteers have said, service within the Peace Corps can be one of the most meaningful experiences you will ever have and, as Peace Corps is fond of saying, it will likely be 'the toughest job you'll ever love.' Millions of people around the world, from politicians to public school students, have said that they believe Peace Corps offers a valuable addition to the great common cause of world development. It has been featured in Hollywood movies (like *Volunteers* starring Tom Hanks); provided formative years for United States Senators and Representatives for decades; provided help to countless men, women, and children throughout the world; and has become a household name in communities throughout every country on the planet. The Peace Corps has a proud past and a bright future, especially with Volunteers like you, who are ready to live with a host community and serve as a trained Volunteer (the first and second goal) while sharing your experiences with everyone you know and love back home (the third goal).

PEACE CORPS JARGON

PCV (Peace Corps Volunteer): Currently completing service
RPCV (Returned Peace Corps Volunteer): Completed service
PCT (Peace Corps Trainee): Currently completing training
PST (Pre-Service Training): 3 months of training before service
HCA (Host Country Agency): Where a Volunteer works
HCN (Host Country National): Citizen where Volunteer serves
IST (In-Service Training): Conference during first year
MST (Mid-Service Training): Conference after first year
COS (Close of Service): Conference at the end of service
Site: Where a Volunteer lives during their service
Site mate: Fellow Volunteers who live nearby
ET (Early Termination): Leaving service voluntarily
NPCA: National Peace Corps Association

To learn more, visit www.TravisHellstrom.com/PeaceCorps101.

About This Handbook

There is a certain cathartic element in writing a handbook like this and it is important for us to admit that outright. We wrote this to benefit you and your Peace Corps journey, but we also write to help us make sense of ours. We aren't perfect Volunteers; we have just had experiences that you might like to hear about. Your Peace Corps experience is unique and we wish you the very best. In fact, this handbook is much more yours than ours, and we have left plenty of space to prove it. This is designed to be an interactive companion for the important thoughts and concerns you may have as a Peace Corps Volunteer. It is meant to be a place for you to explore who you are, to understand the challenges you will face as a Volunteer (all the way from your application to returning home), to hear tips from other Volunteers, and to share your questions and concerns with other people who are also going through their own unique and incredible Peace Corps experiences.

In fact, you should know that this handbook is ultimately useless unless you take ownership of it. Write your name on the front; scribble, doodle, and improve on our methods. Every page and empty space in this book was made specifically with you in mind. We hope it is fun, interactive, and relevant. It has required several years and many people to write this handbook, but the most important moment in the life of this particular book is happening *right now*. As soon as your pen touches this paper, it's yours. It was written just for this purpose and we hope you make the most of it. Thank you for sharing your experience with us. We've started the conversation, and we'd love to hear what you have to say...

A Timeline of Your Peace Corps Experience

Applying to Peace Corps

- Application
- Interview
- Nomination
- Medical Clearance
- Invitation

Preparing for Peace Corps

- Take Time for Yourself
- Say Goodbye to Family & Friends
- Read the Fine Print
- Pack Your Bags

Training for Peace Corps

- Staging Event
- Pre-Service Training
- Language Proficiency
- Swearing-In Ceremony

Your First Year

- Site Placement
- Getting To Know Your New Community
- Adjusting To Your New Life & Work
- In-Service Training
- Project Development Training

Your Second Year

- Community Projects
- Mid-Service Training
- Helping New Volunteers
- Reflecting on Service
- Close of Service Conference

Returning Home

- Talking with RPCVs
- Spending Time with Friends and Family
- Getting Reacquainted with Home

Sargent Shriver, Founding Director of Peace Corps (1961).

APPLYING TO PEACE CORPS

Get To Know Peace Corps

A common question people ask is, "What can I do to become a better Peace Corps applicant?" This is a complicated and wonderful question. To start, it's important to do a lot of research on your own and reach out to people in the Peace Corps community.

Research
There is a tremendous amount of information out there for people who want to learn about Peace Corps: online journals and videos, great books and articles written by Volunteers, and, of course, the enormous Peace Corps website. Flip to the Resources section at the end of this book to see some of our favorite resources and ways to connect to the Peace Corps community. Pay close attention to what you think you might like to do, what areas you could see yourself working in, and what really gets you excited about Peace Corps service.

Attend a Peace Corps Event

To attend an event, visit the Peace Corps website, find your nearest Peace Corps Recruitment office, and check out upcoming events both online and in-person. This is a great chance to meet Returned Peace Corps Volunteers (RPCVs) as well as other people interested in Peace Corps. Keep in mind, it's never too early to do this. The great stories you'll hear and the inspiration you'll find will be contagious. Don't be surprised if you meet Volunteers who you then correspond with for months. They are a diverse and wonderful source of expert advice and personal experience.

Make Yourself Competitive

In addition to meeting people in the Peace Corps community, there are other things you can do to make yourself a better applicant. Whatever your area of interest, Peace Corps is looking for defining characteristics that span across sectors: motivation and commitment, competence in your field, social sensitivity and cultural awareness, and emotional maturity. To prepare for your application—and more importantly to prepare for your Peace Corps service—there are several things you can do to improve in these areas and make yourself a better Volunteer.

Demonstrate Leadership

Exercise your ability to identify challenges and create solutions. Anyone can be a leader and it rarely requires a title or position. Leadership is the ability to influence others by finding your voice and helping others find theirs; seeing others' potential so clearly that they can't help but see it in themselves.

Think about what really matters to you (helping kids, saving the environment, creating a successful business, learning, teaching, *anything*) and then get more passionate about dedicating yourself to those causes. It isn't hard to identify problems; the challenge has always been doing something about them. As you become more passionate at creating solutions, people will be drawn to you and you can begin to work together to make things happen. That takes a leader, a visionary, and the kind of person who will be perfect for Peace Corps.

Commit to Service

Making a decision to serve in Peace Corps for 27 months is a commitment to give over 820 days to serving others—that's almost 20,000 hours of excitement and frustration, hopeful, hopeless, wonderful, and horrible experiences, minute after minute, week after week. The desire to help others will only pull you through this adventure if you are willing to reach deep down inside to ask yourself how much you are really willing to give. Peace Corps will shake your worldview, probably in a very good way, and you can prepare for that now by honestly answering this question, "Do I believe it's important to help others? If so, what am I doing right now to live that out?" Peace Corps service requires a huge heart, and it helps if it's a muscle you've already been working out before you apply.

Develop Understanding

We don't all have the opportunity to study abroad or even leave our country or home state, but we all have the opportunity to leave our comfort zone and do things outside our norm. When we push ourselves, step into a new environment, accept the reality that *the world* is larger than *our world*, and begin to act on that, we develop the skill set essential to any Volunteer: empathy, humility, kindness, flexibility, and strength. Peace Corps is looking for this adaptive ability, since they will uproot you from everything you know and plant you in a completely new and very different place to see how you will survive and grow. With the right mindset, you will astound yourself with your personal growth—guaranteed. To start, try reaching out to those around you, maybe your local international community or club, to build relationships with people from entirely different cultures and backgrounds.

Step 1: The Application

Peace Corps views all the preliminary stuff that a person does as part of the application process, before a person actually goes online and fills out the application. Anything that you do, as far as watching videos of Peace Corps volunteers, speaking to Peace Corps volunteers and return Peace Corps volunteers; any work that you do—going to information sessions, speaking to a recruiter, or just getting psyched about Peace Corps and learning about the organization—is part of the application process.

The Peace Corps application is remarkably thorough, roughly 26 pages, but it can be completed in a week or so if you concentrate. We say just dive right in. There is no harm in starting early on the application and taking your time to get an overview of how it looks. As you start filling out the application, really be yourself. As you'll see later in the interview, your essays and activities will play an important role in the interviewer's impression of who you are.

The Peace Corps Volunteer Application has two parts: simple forms and more detailed sections. While most sections are simple, some deserve a little extra attention and some advice we would like to share. Let's take a look...

When you choose to apply on the Peace Corps website, you can see the openings before you even begin the application process! Go to peacecorps.gov/openings for more information.

Location & Job Preferences
Peace Corps wants to know where you see yourself and what you see yourself doing as a Volunteer. When you first create your account on the Peace Corps website, you will have to choose from a variety of area options and general job preferences before they list the available openings. Go ahead and research each area on the Peace Corps website to get a good idea of what different work assignments mean in areas like Health, Agriculture and Education. Then, make a short list of what you could see yourself doing. Your recruiter will be very excited to talk about where and how you see yourself serving as a

Volunteer, so be prepared to talk with him or her about why you chose your preferences, and be open to their suggestions on both job and area.

Volunteer Openings
The Peace Corps website will list the available openings in the area that offer the jobs you desire. You can sort the options if you chose either "Anything" as a job or "Anywhere" as an area. You can also filter for jobs with certain language requirements or jobs that accept couples. When you find the job you want in the area you desire, you can read a brief overview of the job and then choose to "Apply Now."

Basic Eligibility
Are you over 18 and a U.S. Citizen by birth or naturalization? You will need to answer those questions, and then fill out contact information, attach or write your resume, fill in background information and answer basic education questions.

After the simple stuff is out of the way, you will get to some more detailed sections.

Motivation Statement
The Peace Corps website says, "Please provide a few paragraphs explaining your reasons for wanting to serve as a Peace Corps Volunteer and how you plan to overcome the various challenges associated with Peace Corps service." This is probably the one spot in the application process where most applicants get stuck. People stall on their essay for months with nervousness and over-estimation of their importance. Don't get stuck; just smile, be yourself and write what feels right. This essay is important, but not dire. It is only one slice in your big pizza of an application, so just say what is in your heart. The interviewer and placement officer (who are the two official people who will read them) want to see that you are human, have an understanding of the world around you, and are open-minded, flexible, helpful, caring, excited, and balanced as an individual.

There are no perfect answers for a personal motivation statement, but there is definitely a Peace Corps spirit that former Volunteers (recruiters and staff) are looking for. They want to know what motivates you, what drives you in life and makes you do what you do. What drives you toward Peace Corps and makes you think Peace Corps is the right next step? You don't have to have everything figured out to write this essay; you just need to know where you are and how you want to move forward from right here. Say what you really feel.

Peace Corps will also want to know what happens when you are brought out of your comfort zone and are challenged to see the world in a new way—your maturity and ability to grow in a new environment. Try writing about a time when you adapted and changed yourself to handle a new experience. This can include study abroad experiences, but it can also include leading an organization in your university, handling a new work project or adapting to a new community. Writing about who you were before and after these experiences can be very helpful to a recruiter. Peace Corps knows your two years of service will be similar to these experiences and they want to see how well you did to better predict how well you *will* do in future situations.

Recommendations

Here, you will add three recommendation providers, including their relationship to you, their e-mail addresses and their phone numbers. They will be e-mailed a link to a recommendation form that is approximately three pages long, and they will have as long as they want to complete it. Make sure you know why you are asking the people you have chosen.

First, your recommendations have to come from:

- A current or previous employment supervisor,
- A current or previous volunteer work supervisor, and
- A close friend who has known you at least 2 years

Second, you need to ask people that complement your application. For example, if you mention one of your friends in your motivation statement, then it might be nice to have them write your close friend recommendation. Your application process is your own and only you will know when it is the right time to ask for recommendations and who to ask to write them.

Once those recommendations have been turned in, you are that much closer to your interview! Congratulations! You will have to fill in a page about Racial and Ethnic Data, confirm your application, do a quick review, and then officially send your application!

Step 2: The Interview

Congratulations again on getting your application in. Now it's time for your interview. The interview is not an interrogation! It really is an opportunity to allow you to elaborate on what you've written in your application, for the recruiter to clarify any confusion, and to really get to know who you are. You are likely wondering, "What will the recruiter ask me and what can I do to prepare for the questions?" First, treat this like a conversation between you and someone who loves the Peace Corps. On the next page, we've included a list of questions recruiters often ask; however, remember that these questions usually come up naturally in a conversation. Look at this less as a time for you to answer questions directed at you and more as a time for you to talk about Peace Corps with someone who has great experience and information. It will be much more comfortable for you both and will likely be a welcome change of pace for your recruiter as well.

Take your time in looking over the following questions and think about what you would like to share with your recruiter in response to them, but definitely *don't* script any answers. The questions are geared toward figuring out who you are and what you have gone through in your life to get you to where you are. Be honest and open about yourself, and be ready to explore your life with someone who is very interested in you. We hope your interview is a great experience for you; it was for us. Dress nicely, relax, and have fun!

Questions Your Recruiter May Ask

- What makes you interested in the Peace Corps?
- Why do you think you will be a good Peace Corps Volunteer?
- What are your plans after serving in the Peace Corps and how does Peace Corps service fit into your long-term plans?
- What, if anything, might keep you from completing a 27-month commitment to Peace Corps service?
- What kind of support do you have from your family and friends regarding serving in the Peace Corps?
- Are you currently in a relationship?
- Please tell me about a time when you had to work in an unstructured environment.
- Please tell me about a successful experience you've had in a leadership role.
- Please tell me about an experience when you were able to transfer some knowledge or skill to someone else.
- Please tell me about a time when you worked with someone different from yourself toward a common goal.
- Can you tell me about a frustrating experience you have had when working with others? How did you manage that frustration?
- What do you do if someone runs something differently than how you would? How do you usually resolve conflicts?
- Have you studied a second language? If so, what challenges did you face and what level of facility did you achieve?
- How do you help others to become better leaders?
- How do you deal with isolation? How about over-crowding and lack of privacy?
- What is the longest you have been physically separated from important people in your life (such as family, friends, or romantic interests)?

- What situations do you typically find stressful? What do you currently do to relieve stress? What do you do for fun?
- When you are overseas, circumstances and/or cultural norms may prevent you from employing your usual ways of managing stress, boredom, and loneliness. You will also most likely be out of touch with your familiar support group.
  - In such a situation, what alternative outlets might you use?
  - If your support group plays a critical role in helping you cope with stress, how will you manage without them?
- Why did you pick your regional and job preferences? How would you rank your flexibility in your preferences, from 1 to 10?
- Do you have food preferences (e.g. vegetarian)? How do you think you will adapt to food, clothing, and environmental comfort changes?
- In some countries, tattoos, body piercings, or unusual hairstyles may be culturally unacceptable. To be a successful Volunteer in such a country, you would have to modify your appearance so that it conforms to local norms. Are you willing to make such an adjustment? Give an example of a time when you had to modify your appearance.
- The following are issues that you may face in your country of service. Do you have any concerns?
  - Different and/or lack of familiar foods
  - Different living conditions
  - Lack of privacy/isolation
  - Prescribed gender roles
  - Possible minority challenges
  - Personal religious requirements/possible lack of access to your own religious services
  - Living in a culture where alcohol may be widely consumed and accepted/living in a culture that prohibits the use of alcohol altogether

Questions We Asked Our Recruiters

An equally important part of the interview is what you ask your recruiter. Be excited about talking to them. They are often very recently Returned Peace Corps Volunteers (RPCVs) and they have gone through everything you will. Your recruiter will probably tell story after story about their Peace Corps experience and you may really enjoy their insight. They are usually in their mid-twenties and they remember what it was like to be in your position as an applicant. Be appreciative and receptive to what they have to say, and feel free to ask what's on your mind, whether it is a question about electricity or a concern you've wanted to address. When your recruiter tells you, "I am here to help you," know that they mean it. He or she can be a huge advocate for you and they are here to help you. Also, be sure to send a note or e-mail to them after the interview to say thanks.

- What was your experience like in the Peace Corps?
- Why did you become a recruiter?
- Could you tell me a little about yourself? Your background? Your interests?
- Who have been some of the best examples of Peace Corps Volunteers that you've met?
- What kind of flexibility and cooperativeness should I expect in the placement process?
- * What did you like most about the Peace Corps?
- What was your most exciting project that you worked on?
- What was most challenging for you?
- * What do you wish you had done in my position during this part in the Peace Corps process?
- What advice do you have as I go through these next steps?

PCV Travis writes, "*In my interview, my recruiter told me, 'In every interview I am basically asking myself, 'Would my host country be lucky to have this Volunteer?' If yes, I nominate them. If no, I don't.*"

It is a beautiful sentiment and one that many recruiters probably agree with. They love Peace Corps and the people that they served as

Volunteers, so they want to pick the very best people to serve their friends and join their ranks as colleagues. Keep this in mind during your interview, and if you honor it, you will be fine.

Step 3: Nomination

Isn't it incredible how fast things are moving? Not too long ago you were finishing your application, and now you are nominated for service in the Peace Corps! Nomination is essentially a recommendation that your recruiter thinks you're a quality applicant and you should be evaluated further, which means going through a medical evaluation, legal evaluation, before finally being considered for placement.

Once you've received the official notification from your recruiter you will move on to the next step in the process: Medical Clearance. Nomination means that your recruiter believes you would make a good Peace Corps Volunteer and they will send your full application on to headquarters in Washington, D.C. for processing. This is also where your recruiter may ask for some more information to be included in your file, such as copies of certifications. Be sure to send in this information as soon as possible. You will also have to get copies of your fingerprints made for your file. You can get this done easily at your local police office.

Now the last two steps in your Peace Corps application process take place. Once the application arrives in Washington, D.C., a medical officer and placement officer will be assigned to your file. The medical officer will send you your Medical Clearance packet for completion (Step 4) and when your packet has been completed and approved by your medical officer, you will be considered for placement (Step 5). You're almost there!

Step 4: Medical Clearance

Up until now, things have probably moved pretty fast, but get ready for a slow down. It's not a bad thing; it's just the way things work during this part of the process. Medical Clearance is the process of checking your medical and dental history and being approved by the Peace Corps Medical Office. By going through a check-up at both your family physician and dentist's offices, Peace Corps gets a look at your overall health and well-being. They want to make sure you are capable of living in the challenging locations you may be placed in, and they will also want records of your health for the healthcare they will provide you during your service.

When your medical forms arrive in the mail, be patient as you look through them—they will be thick. Make your medical appointments as soon as you can—one for your dentist and one for your physician. Explain to them that you are getting a check-up for service in the Peace Corps, and when you arrive at your doctor's and dentist's offices, have all of your forms in hand. You will need to fill out the first sheet or two in the packet, but your health professional will need to fill out the rest. They will date and sign the forms, including necessary shot records, x-rays (digital and film are both okay for dental clearance), and necessary blood tests. Your packet will be even thicker by the end of your check-ups, but by then your part in the medical clearance process will likely be complete.

Send in your forms in the envelope Peace Corps provided for you and you are all set. They will get back to you if you need any additional work done, but once you've been medically cleared, you're on your way to placement!

Can I get rejected?

It's true that Peace Corps applications can be "rejected." Peace Corps headquarters can remove applicants from the pile of nominations before they get an invitation to serve. This can happen for a variety of reasons that are outside your control, including medical reasons.

The best thing for you to do as an applicant is to be respectful, prompt, patient, enthusiastic, and flexible. Once you've been nominated, Peace Corps will do everything it can to place you in a country and job that is a good fit for you. If you handle all interactions respectfully, fill out and send in all requested information promptly, wait patiently (the process *can* be tedious), and remain enthusiastic and flexible about your service, you will have done your best to be placed and invited to serve.

Step 5: Invitation

This is it, the last step in the process to becoming a Peace Corps Volunteer! It is very important to remember to be patient and accept that it might take a while to get your official invitation to serve. Everything in your file must be completed, after which it will all be reviewed by your placement officer—every bit of it. They will consider where your recruiter nominated you for (your region) and what they nominated you to do (your assignment). Then, they will compare that to what current regions and assignments are available. This *does* mean that not all placements match their initial nomination. Don't worry if you get an invitation that you weren't expecting; you can always talk with your placement officer and share your concerns. They are trying to do what is best for your future Peace Corps post as well as what is best for you as a future Volunteer.

After you receive your invitation, you have 10 days to decide if you will accept it. Call your placement officer and let them know what you think. Once you've accepted, you are all set for departure. You have moved all the way from interest in the Peace Corps to an invitation to serve within the organization!

We wish you the very best in your journey! You have worked hard to get to where you are and you deserve it. We hope you really enjoy your two years of service within one of the greatest organizations in the world. Your adventure is only beginning...

Should I accept my invitation?
It's hard to know how to respond to your invitation at first. There is such a mix of excitement, nervousness, and urgency. First, remember you have 10 days from when you receive the invitation to accept it, so take your time. Second, remember you have a lot of people you can rely on to answer your questions and provide you with advice. These include family and friends, RPCVs and PCVs that are currently in

the field, and Peace Corps staff as well. Google "Peace Corps" and "Your Country" and look for Volunteers through PeaceCorpsJournals.com, Facebook groups, and other resources listed in the back of this handbook to see what they think. Talk with RPCVs you may have met in person through information sessions, other friends, and chance meetings. Not only are Peace Corps Volunteers often very friendly people, they are usually brutally honest, if you want them to be. Read their blogs, e-mail them, message them on Facebook, and then consider their replies. Also, when sending out e-mails to Volunteers in the field, make sure you e-mail enough people that you are likely to get a few replies in your 10-day window (some PCVs don't have regular internet access for weeks at a time). Lastly, follow your heart. Whatever direction you feel called to go, talk it out with your Placement Officer and let them know what you think.

What happens if I decline an invitation?

Generally speaking, Peace Corps is going to try and work with you if you really feel like you need to decline your invitation. However, officially a second invitation is never a guarantee. When you call your Placement Officer to decline your invitation, they will want a detailed explanation of why you are declining. They may want this explanation on the phone or will request you send them an e-mail. Remember your Placement Officer is trying to do what is best for the Peace Corps country post where they need you *and* what is best for you as a Volunteer. Spend a few days thinking over your decision, discussing it with your friends, family, and other PCVs and RPCVs (especially in that country), and make a list of reasons why you *do* and *do not* want to serve in that country. When you speak with your Placement Officer, try to do so with an open mind and make sure you understand one another. If you decide to decline, be ready to explain those reasons and then only expect one more invitation.

What's next?

Your next step is filling out your passport and visa forms, as well as your aspiration and resume forms, for your country desk. The passport and visa forms are to be sent back to the Peace Corps as soon as you can in the envelopes they have included. Then your aspiration statement and resume are sent into your country desk by e-mail so that your future Peace Corps staff can get to know who you are and place you well in your future job once you arrive (and have gone through training).

I accepted! I have so many questions!

You will be astounded by the incredible answers that you can get from other Volunteers, both those who are in your destination country and those who have already served there. There are a lot of incredible resources available for incoming Peace Corps Volunteers. Definitely check out the helpful resources listed in the back of this handbook—they are full of great information.

Search for groups online or start your own. You will be amazed by how many people will respond to your questions on Facebook discussion boards. Current and past Volunteers are often very welcoming and honest about what to expect and how to prepare for leaving. Online groups are also a great chance to meet the Volunteers you will be serving with when you leave. If you read a great PCV blog on a place like PeaceCorpsJournals.com, send the PCV an e-mail. Individual Volunteers would probably love to hear from you and they can be very helpful and motivating. It's very likely they remember feeling the same way you do now.

Now that you have completed your application, finished your interview, been nominated, passed medical clearance, and accepted your invitation, it's time to move onto the next big stage in your adventure: Preparing for Peace Corps...

MY NOTES

PREPARING FOR PEACE CORPS

The Important Stuff

Before leaving for Peace Corps, it can be an incredible feeling to do something you have always wanted to do but didn't have time to do. Especially if that something has always been in your heart, but maybe your head has always said, "Not now." The time between receiving your invitation and leaving to serve could be weeks or months. Take some of that time to relax and do incredible things you love. Take a hike with a friend, take a workshop or two, learn some things you always wanted to learn—they might inform more areas of your life than you can imagine and later, during your service, you will be very glad you did them. Spend plenty of quality time with your friends and family. They can be a huge source of support during your service and it's nice to thank them ahead of time.

More than all the peanut butter and pizza in the world, we bet you'll miss your family and friends the most. Spend as much time as you can with them before you leave the country. It might be a year, 27 months, or more before you see them again. Say what you need to say. Give everyone hugs. Tell them you will talk to them soon, either through e-mail, Skype, or good old-fashioned paper and pencil inside a little white envelope. When you arrive at in-country, you'll figure out which one will work best.

Meditation Retreat

The word 'meditation' conjures up a lot of different thoughts in people's minds, but for individuals who have attended a meditation retreat, they will probably say it was 'incredible.' It can share invaluable lessons about perception, sensation, the space between you and your mind, patience, pain and pleasure (and the destructive power of both), and most of all, your weaknesses and your strengths. "*The retreat I went on was one of the most incredible experiences of my life,*" writes PCV Travis, "*and it was a great way to prepare me for my Peace Corps service.*"

Retreats can inspire you to think about your life in a new way, and put you into a great receptive state, so that you are ready to take in the unique and incredible world of a Volunteer. If you have the time before leaving for Peace Corps, consider signing up for a free Vipassanna meditation retreat, which you can learn about in the Resources section of your handbook.

Learning how to slow down is a huge advantage in the Peace Corps. College and jobs in America can be very fast-paced and it will be hard to slow down at first, but spending some time not doing anything at all can be quite helpful. Something like a retreat could be one of the best things you have ever done and can prepare you for the Peace Corps in ways you could never imagine.

Anticipate Achieving Your Fitness Goals

Peace Corps Volunteers can experience great weight change during their service—some lose weight, some gain weight. In some Peace Corps posts, men tend to lose weight and women to gain weight, while in other posts the opposite is true. If you contact PCVs and

RPCVs ahead of time, they will probably tell you what you might expect in your host country.

"*Walking into Peace Corps, I weighed 255 pounds and I had been out of shape for a long time,*" writes PCV Travis, "*Within my first year I had dropped down to 195 and gotten into the best shape of my life. It was a wonderful feeling and the time, space and lifestyle I had during Peace Corps helped make that happen.*"

Whatever the case is for you, know that the new environment, eating habits, and traditional foods that you encounter during your Peace Corps service can be a huge asset. Think about what getting into better shape would look like for you and know that it is totally achievable in Peace Corps. Plan for it. Bring some clothes that you can fit into if you get into better shape or be ready to ask your friends and family to send you new clothes. Weight change can be a very good thing and getting into better shape is always great. It will be wonderful for your health and will make you feel incredible. Be ready to encourage this by having clothes that you love to wear or maybe ones that you've always *wanted* to wear!

"*Working out for me became not only an important part for my physical health, but my mental health, too!*" writes PCV Bonnie. "*I noticed that I had far more energy to invest in projects and my students after I started taking care of myself more. It even led to a class discussion on health when my students started to notice that I had slimmed down.*"

Read the Fine Print

If you didn't already know it, you *are* on the Peace Corps radar. They are watching you, but not in a bad way. You will hear about this plenty of times during your service, but we better just cover it here: Peace Corps requires that you place a disclaimer on all of your online materials while in Peace Corps which states: "The views on this site are personal and do not in any way reflect those of the Peace Corps." This is similar to any other large organization that has many employees.

We are, probably more than any other generation, very technologically savvy. We have a continual presence online, especially on sites like Facebook, Blogger, and Wordpress. This is an incredible thing, as we all know, because it allows us unprecedented connectedness with our friends and family.

It is also something we have to be cautious about. Anything you put online can be read by anyone. This seems obvious, but it's easy to forget. Expect your Peace Corps Country Director or Placement Officer to read or watch whatever blog posts, videos, group wall comments, or messages you post online. It's part of their job now. E-mails and certain conversations can be private and candid, but anything else is up for grabs.

Before you arrive in country, current Volunteers and staff probably know way more about you than you think. Don't be surprised to hear them say, "Oh, you are so-and-so..." As excited as you are to arrive for your new Peace Corps experience, current PCVs might be even more excited for you to join them. They will watch your You-Tube videos, follow you on Facebook, and answer your questions in discussion boards. When you first meet your Country Director and they say, "We've been talking about you," don't be surprised.

It's great to share your experiences with others, both Volunteers and friends and family back home. If there isn't one already started, putting together a Facebook group for your batch of Volunteers can be really helpful and a great way to get to know people before staging, training, and service. Consider a name like "Peace Corps Philippines (126)," which would be the 126th group to serve in the Philippines, to be able to talk with people going into service with you at the same time. The discussion boards will fill like crazy and people will have a lot to talk about in the weeks and months leading up to your departure.

For people back home in the United States, it can be very fascinating to hear about what you do in the Peace Corps. You may hear a lot of people say, "I would love to do the Peace Corps." It's something that is adventurous and exciting and they'll love to hear your thoughts, watch your videos, see your pictures, and read your stuff online. Lots of incredible things can happen when you post things, including partnerships, donations, helping others, and achieving that Third Goal—helping promote a better understanding of other peoples on the part of all Americans.

It's never too late to do the Peace Corps and you never know who you'll inspire.

If you aren't sure whether you should put something online, ask an older Volunteer or staff member. They know what can and can't go up and it's always better to check. Also, you can't put up the Peace Corps logo, but you can use images from the Peace Corps website (like web banners) and you can buy logo stuff from the National Peace Corps Association (NPCA).

Peace Corps, like any U.S. government organization, is concerned about its image not only in America but also around the world. By watching what is put online, they are safeguarding America's reputation and the future of the program. Just remember and honor the fact that you are an ambassador for America and the Peace Corps, and you should be fine.

Two Years and Change

Two years and two months. That's how long the famous American writer Henry David Thoreau was at Walden Pond. It's probably no coincidence that many Peace Corps Volunteers see a correlation between what Thoreau did and what many of us are doing during our service:

"I went to the woods because I wished to live deliberately," Thoreau writes to start his book, *"to front only the essential facts of life, and see if I could not learn what it had to teach, and not, when I came to die, discover that I had not lived."*

We spend two years and three months of our lives facing life in a much more raw way than many Americans ever choose to. We do it deliberately because we believe in it and we hope to come out the other side wiser and better people. In Peace Corps, there is an incredible amount of time for introspection into who we are, what is important in life, and what the world has to teach us if we are awake to it.

"I have never met a man who was quite awake," Thoreau writes in his closing lines, *"Only that day dawns to which we are awake."*

"This is the time to awake, while you are young and strong."
Buddha

Your "All-Important" Sector

It will be easy to get wrapped up in your job title and to think that your Peace Corps service will be defined by your sector. We know it's one of very few things you have to go on in that little invitation packet of yours, but keep in mind that every Peace Corps Volunteer, regardless of sector, is a Peace Corps Volunteer. Your challenges and frustrations will be shared with people across sectors and across the world. The more you see yourself as part of the larger Peace Corps community, the better off you probably will be. Sure, our jobs and our workplaces differ. Some of us have summer vacation, some of us have full-time translators, some of us have rigorous work schedules, and some of us have advanced graduate degrees. But in more ways than one, everyone gets put on the same level playing field and the things that separate a happy Volunteer from an unhappy Volunteer have a lot more to do with mindset and character than a job description and resume. Enjoy your sector, but more importantly, enjoy your job: helping others.

Pack Light and Fun

Many PCVs look back and think they packed way, way, *way* too much stuff.

"Pack light. I mean really, really light. You'll be so glad you did," says PCV Scott. *"Limit yourself to two bags. Bring bags that you can actually use beyond initially arriving in country. I packed two bags inside a duffel, which worked great. Don't forget the fun. Things like music, books, a Frisbee, journals, and games go a long, long way."*

Don't worry about books on the native language (Peace Corps

will have plenty for you), but bring some nice clothes, rechargeable batteries and charger if you need them, and if you're a music lover, bring a device that can withstand the elements (and maybe a head-phone splitter so you can share your music with your neighbor on those long bus rides). If you are wondering about bringing your lap-top, bring it. It's definitely worth it. Don't forget your system disks or repair software. Most of the time you'll be your own repair person if something happens to your computer, so be prepared.

You may have an urge to pack 500 Q-tips and industrial size shampoos, but don't. Give your new host country's people credit; they have cool stuff of their own. Use that valuable luggage weight for things like books you've always wanted to read and an external hard drive to swap movie and books with other Volunteers...you will be glad you did.

"*My main advice*," says PCV Scott, "*is to pack light, pack light, and pack light.*"

Clear Your Mind

Be patient, be flexible, and have as few expectations as possible as you walk onto the plane. It will be easier to go with the flow if you don't have pre-conceived notions about what the experience will be like. Everyone's experience in a country is different.

"*Be patient (everything moves much slower in Peace Corps) and be flexible,*" writes PCV Scott. "*Realize that you are living in a foreign land and culture. Don't expect things to always go the way you had planned. Most likely, things won't go your way most of the time. Just roll with it.*"

You have probably heard this from PCVs and RPCVs, but rein in your expectations and get ready for an experience that will be unlike anything you can imagine. As you get on the plane and head out to staging, be mindful and have an open mind. Oh, and be kind and friendly too...that always helps.

"*It is better to travel well than to arrive.*"
BUDDHA

MY NOTES

_____

_____

_____

_____

_____

_____

_____

_____

_____

_____

_____

_____

_____

_____

_____

_____

_____

_____

_____

_____

_____

_____

_____

_____

_____

_____

_____

_____

_____

TRAINING FOR PEACE CORPS

Being Yourself

You are starting your staging event! We are so excited for you and hope you have a really wonderful time. PCV Mark writes, *"Be your true self, right from the beginning. It's going to come out eventually, so just start out that way."* There may be a lot of drama and comedy over the next few months of Pre-Service Training within your group, but some of the best things you can do are smile, relax, and be yourself. It is okay to be flexible and try new things, but don't feel like you have to re-invent yourself. If you're a wonderful person, everyone will figure that out sooner or later.

Also, rather than giving in to the gossip machine, focus on talking with people and getting to know them, appreciating their strengths and forgiving their weaknesses. There will be all kinds of people in your group and it may be tempting to label them. Instead, just try to care about them and be a friend to everyone you can. *"Be yourself from the beginning (a joker, a quiet type, an independent type, loud, talkative, whatever),"* writes PCV Mark, *"and people will see you as being true to yourself. It makes a good impression to act normal—whatever normal is for you."*

High Fives Off The Plane

"Chances are good when you step off the plane in your host country, you will have to walk through a column of cheering and screaming PCVs at the airport," writes PCV Mark, *"You will make a good impression if you are effortlessly moving around with your stuff. It is one of the first impressions people have when they see you. Being able to look people right in the eye and give some high fives because your luggage is not too cumbersome is pretty awesome. People will see you as more confident and self-sufficient if you can walk a half mile comfortably with your load, your hands are somewhat free, and you can even help other people in the group."*

Being able to shake hands and give high fives is another great reason to pack light. All the current Volunteers will be excited to see you and meet you; you will certainly understand the feeling next year when you are meeting the new Volunteers yourself.

The 27-Month Cycle

On the one hand, it is kind of ridiculous to say that there is a "timeline" that you are going to go through as a Volunteer. We are sticking to our story that every Peace Corps Volunteer and their experience is unique. On the other hand, it can be helpful to refer to the resources that other Volunteers have created to summarize their experiences for the benefit of others. The book you hold in your hands is one such resource; *A Few Minor Adjustments* by Peace Corps is another we highly recommend, and another created some years ago by Volunteers finishing their service in Senegal is a helpful tool they called the "27-Month Cycle." We have included a copy of it in the Resources at the end of this handbook, and left some space so you can add your own thoughts.

You may find it surprising and comforting to see that other Volunteers feel similarly at different stages of service—we all face similar challenges in posts around the world. We hope that keeping the different stages in mind not only gives you insight into your own experience, but into the experiences of other Volunteers around you as well.

Avoid Judgments

"If you judge people, you have no time to love them."
MOTHER TERESA

In general, avoid comparing yourself and your experience to other Volunteers. Peace Corps staff, host country nationals, and other PCVs will already be doing this for you. To stay sane, concentrate on how to do the best job you can, given your situation and the skills you have and can learn. With that being said, don't be afraid to stretch yourself, and *do* ask others for advice if something in your experience seems "off".

When you first arrive at Staging and Pre-Service Training (PST), it will be very tempting to label people. Don't. People are much more interesting and incredible than any labels we can give them. Aren't you? Try hard to appreciate everything you can about the people around you, and to look inside yourself to find out if the thing that bothers you about someone else is actually something that bothers you about yourself. Be the change you wish to see in the world, not the guy or girl who points his or her finger and tells someone else to change.

"I think in a very natural way, all of the PCV's in my group were looking for people to immediately group with during that first week of training," writes PCV Bonnie. *"And a lot of great friendships formed that way. But don't be closed off to accepting the friendships that will come out of your training group, your new sites mates, and even the new volunteers when you are starting your second year."*

Learn How to Wait

> *"Nature does not hurry, yet everything is accomplished."*
> LAO TZU

Patience and flexibility. You will hear those words again and again during training. Learning how to wait and embracing it takes time. Getting annoyed or angry over how long things are taking is something you have to deprogram in your mind. Reading, writing, meditating, and talking are great things you can do while you wait. Play to your talents and passions. If you love writing, carry writing materials with you. If you love reading, carry books. If music, carry your favorite device…whatever it is that you love to do, have that ready so that no moment feels wasted. It's also always nice to bring an open mind and listening ear which could really make the day for the person next to you. Be open to the fact that, very often, you will have no control over when things happen.

"*I was trying to explain the word 'patience',*" writes PCV Travis, "*and the best thing I could come up with in my limited Mongolian was: it's like waiting, but being happy while you wait. Growing up in America I always thought of 'being patient' as something that I had to do until I got what I wanted. But after Peace Corps, I realized happy and waiting doesn't fit that. It isn't about getting what I want at all— it's about being happy with whatever I have.*"

Be Thoughtful

> *The best effect of fine persons is felt after we have left their presence."*
> RALPH WALDO EMERSON

PCV Mark, who was also a PST Trainer, offers this bit of advice, "*Be courteous and helpful to other trainees and Peace Corps staff from the moment you arrive at staging until the end of your training. You are being evaluated from the first day by your trainers, the other trainees, and staff. Be calm. Be smart. Be resourceful and thoughtful.*

Also, when in large groups during your training and there is a Question & Answer time, always ask yourself this before you let your question loose: 'Is the answer to my question going to benefit the group if I ask it at this time?' If yes, then fire away. If no, try to ask the person later one-on-one."

Applying this filter is something others will really appreciate. Everyone is nervous, experiencing lots of changes, and filled with lots of questions. Just be patient and look out for the other people in the group.

PCV Bonnie notes, *"When I first arrived, I was too shy to speak up in groups. Waiting to ask my questions one on one, rather than in front of the whole group, was not only more comfortable for me, but it allowed me to have great conversations and interactions with the trainers and staff. And it let everyone else get out of the session sooner too!"*

A Club of Club Presidents

"I can learn from every man and in that he is my superior."
HENRY DAVID THOREAU

You will probably see this on day one of training: in Peace Corps, you are surrounded by people who are leaders, presidents of this, and organizers of that...you are all outstanding people in surprising ways. Maybe it's the nature of the job that Peace Corps attracts those kinds of characters. It's at once humbling and inspiring to be part of such an incredible group of people. Learn what you can from everyone, honor the potential of all the future Volunteers surrounding you, and realize how much you have to offer one another. Peace Corps (and life, for that matter) is a collaborative effort, and the more you help one another, the better off everyone will be.

"Bond with your roommates and enjoy opening up and being honest as soon as you can," writes PCV Mark. *"The people you train with are*

going to learn all about you anyhow. Often times, the secrets, fears, and doubts we try to conceal are the ones people find the fastest—or under the most embarrassing or tragic times. Be honest!"

Language Learning

"If you talk to a man in a language he understands,
that goes to his head. If you talk to him in his own language,
that goes to his heart."
NELSON MANDELA

Language training in the Peace Corps is highly regarded outside the organization as one of the most effective methods of learning a foreign language. Peace Corps has taught hundreds of languages and no matter where you serve, you will learn one of them. The tricky part is that you will learn this new language while also going to cross-cultural classes, job sector training, adjusting to personal and interpersonal dynamics that spring up in your new environment, and having a well-meaning host family that tries to guide you every step of the way. This will already be a stressful situation and it's no wonder that language can take a backseat to the many other things happening from day to day.

With that being said, just try your best to learn the language basics during training, study when you can, and definitely take advantage of the free time you have with your host family to practice your language skills. This will pay off in the long run and will make your service much easier. It can help you more deeply experience the new culture you find yourself in, perform better in your new job as a Volunteer, and adjust more quickly to your new environment at site. It's fine to relax and enjoy a few games of Solitaire or watch an episode of your favorite show on your laptop every now and then; just smile when your host sister bounds into your room wanting to play Uno again or your host family wants to have a conversation about American pizza. Flip through those Peace Corps dictionaries like a maniac, act out how you feel in the never-ending game of charades, and know that around the world other Peace Corps Volunteers are smiling, knowing just how you feel.

Not Dropping Out

When someone asks why people drop out of Peace Corps, many Volunteers respond, "It isn't exactly dropping out." Peace Corps isn't high school, and suggesting that it's always bad to leave your service fails to take into account the myriad reasons why leaving could be a very good decision for many Volunteers. We can't enumerate all of them here since there are too many, but we will just say that it's important to let go of any taboo you feel toward leaving the Peace Corps. It is an intensely personal experience and, like each of our individual lives, it is often much better to just focus on our own challenges and ask ourselves if we are making the right decision.

When thinking about leaving the Peace Corps early, give yourself plenty of time to think it over, several days at least. Really rough patches in Peace Corps service can sometimes last longer than a few days or a week or two. Talk with a variety of people you trust and admire, and don't just limit yourself to current Volunteers in-country. Feel free to contact your close friends back in America as well as Volunteers in other countries around the world. Your situation is unique, but you will probably be surprised by how similar your experience might be to that of other Volunteers. Finally, while it may sound cheesy, do what feels right in your heart. Regardless of all the valuable feedback you get from the people you care most about, no one else can make this decision for you. Trust yourself.

Also, keep in mind when you tell Peace Corps you are ready to leave, they won't keep you waiting. You could be on a flight back to America within two days. It can happen very quickly, so tell them when you are sure you're ready to go.

Volunteering for Psychological Difficulty

A general rule of Peace Corps is that you are going to run into psychological difficulties, whether you call them barriers, opportunities, frustrations, stress, or any other number of names. In fact, Peace Corps service could easily be compared to an intense self-awareness retreat. You will have the time and space to learn about yourself in ways that will probably astound you. This can be incredibly inspiring and surprisingly frustrating. Both are completely reasonable.

"There will definitely be challenges and frustrating days and weeks," writes PCV Scott. *"Do the best you can and remember how cool it is— what you are doing, where you are living, and what you are a part of."*

Be sure to share your thoughts and frustrations with other Volunteers you trust and admire, including Volunteers in other countries. You have a lot on your mind and a lot going on, but try to focus on just where you are and make the most of that time, wherever it is. It will move past quickly and you can't get it back. It will be tempting to think ahead to all of the things to come, and to wish for things to be over with—whether it's language tests, interviews, training programs, or maybe your daily language classes. Believe it or not, you will probably look back fondly on this time and either be glad you made the most of it or wish you had. For all its foibles, PST is a wonderful time with tons of friends, helpful language classes and job training, and preparation for what you need to know at site. Know that your Trainers, Peace Corps staff, your Language and Cultural Facilitators, your host families, and host communities are watching everything you say and do very carefully. That's another reason to just relax and be yourself.

Be yourself. You will always be the second best anyone else.

Site Placement

Finding out your future site and swearing in as a bona fide Volunteer is a very exciting time. Remember, you don't need to be in a particular job or particular place to be happy. Getting what you want could be one of the worst things that could happen, and conversely, getting what you think you don't want could be one of the best things that ever happened to you. It all depends on how you handle it and how you look at it. The toughest assignments are often the ones that change people the most and that people hold closest to their hearts.

Before you leave for site, you and your new supervisor will talk things through and get to know one another a little bit. Here are some expectations our supervisors had of us as Volunteers:

- Be open-minded, adaptable, tolerant, patient, and kind
- Be creative, hardworking, sensitive, and a team player
- Stay clean and dress well
- Make a lot of good relationships with neighbors and others
- Participate in community sports, activities, and events
- Study, learn, improve your knowledge, and share it
- Be honest and share your concerns with counterparts
- Be friendly, a leader, and a good example
- Recognize that you are seen as a role model at all times
- Review English in documents and websites
- Help use equipment like projectors and printers
- Share American culture and celebrations
- Help and encourage adults in the community
- Share American problem-solving techniques
- Be flexible in situations and choose your battles carefully
- Identify challenges and be patient with identifying fixes

MY NOTES

MAKING THE MOST OF YOUR SERVICE

Same Here

There is an old story of two travelers coming into a new town to live. The first traveler comes up to the entrance of the town and meets an old man. The traveler asks, "I'm new, what are the people here like?"

The old man smiles and asks, "Well, what were the people in your old town like?"

"In the town where I come from the people were lazy, mean, stupid, horrible," the first traveler replies, "I had to leave and find somewhere better."

The old man smiles and says, "It's the same here."

"I figured," says the man before he continues walking.

The second traveler comes to the entrance of the town and sees the old man.

He asks the same question, "I'm new here, what are the people in this town like?"

The old man smiles again, "Well, what were the people in your old town like?"

"In the town where I come from the people were friendly and worked hard," responds the second traveler, "It was a wonderful place and difficult to leave."

The old man smiles and replies, "It's the same here."

Being Kind and Assertive

Walking into your new job as a Peace Corps Volunteer will be intimidating for lots of reasons, and one of the biggest will be defining your role in your new workplace. Time and again during your service it will become clear that you work *with* your organization, but you don't work *for* them. Your salary, your responsibilities, and your support system span Peace Corps and your new host country agency. Your colleagues include host country nationals in your office as well as your community members and your fellow Peace Corps Volunteers. The idea that "all Peace Corps Volunteers are community development volunteers" might be difficult for your colleagues to understand at first, but it is an important part of our jobs.

PCV Travis writes this story about his first week at site:

"In the first week of my service I sat down with my director for the first time, surrounded by a half dozen of the most powerful people in our state hospital. After pleasantries, she looked at the work plan that my new supervisor and I had written during the final days of training before coming to site.

'I don't understand this,' she said. 'I want you to write a new one.'

'Also,' she continued, looking me directly in the eye, 'Do you work at the hospital or in the community?'

As she said this, she pointed to the parts of the work plan that included me working with the local schools, the children's center, and the local university alongside my fellow Volunteers. Having never spoken to my director before, and judging by the intense stares from everyone else at the conference table, I knew this was going to be a very important moment in our relationship. In retrospect, it was an important moment in my relationships with everyone at the table. These people would later become my closest friends, counterparts, and allies. I smiled at her with every ounce of kindness I had in me and spoke in the simple Mongolian I knew, "I work in the hospital and I work in the community. Together." Then, not sure if that would cut it, I added, "Peace Corps says."

All the stares quickly moved from me to my director, who continued to stare at me. After a few moments, she burst out laughing. Everyone smiled, especially me, and she continued with a laugh that I would hear for the next two years and learn to love.

"Okay," she said, touching my shoulder. "That sounds good."

If you want to work some time in your office and some time outside it, be clear, kind, and assertive about your position as a Volunteer. Enjoying your job is much easier when you do what you love, no matter where it takes you. Even if you need to say, "Peace Corps says."

Making Work Work for You

Peace Corps is a unique work environment because it allows you to set out how, when, and why you want to work. Sometimes, you'll be able to choose some of these, in full or in part.

One of the first times you will be tested is in your first week on the job. You may be in a school, a hospital, a chamber of commerce, or many other places, but in that first week, and even in your first month, you have the priceless opportunity to set out your style, your work ethic, work schedule, and your personal expectations between you and your workplace. Prepare yourself for this however you like (whether by writing out your goals, talking with your friends, writing out a weekly schedule, or thinking about times in your life when you were happiest and why) and know that you will be tested by your coworkers and bosses in particular. If you give up control of your time to someone else, remember *you* are giving up control. This is *your* life and *your* Peace Corps experience. Going to work and sitting at a desk because that's what everyone else does is easy but it isn't nearly as fun as deciding for yourself when and why you are going to work. Here are some questions to consider:

- How many hours a week would you like to be in the office, ideally?
- Can you communicate with your counterparts that you can work effectively outside of the office, like at your home (that might have internet access)?
- How do you stay motivated to achieve your goals?
- Do you feel comfortable asserting yourself and deciding what you do and do not want to spend your time doing at work?

Things to Remember

- It's true that you work in a school, hospital, or organization, but you are first and foremost a Peace Corps Volunteer. You may work in an office, but you don't have to work everyone else's office hours. In fact, you rarely should. Community development—a priority of every Volunteer regardless of sector—doesn't usually fall between office hours, and certainly doesn't always take place in the office. Go out into the community, work on joint projects with other sectors, volunteer with international organizations like Scouts or the Red Cross, and know that it's okay to tell your office you're not coming in that afternoon.

- Make your job clear with your supervisors. Host agencies can be possessive and unsure of your exact role in the organization. It is up to you to decide what that is. If they ask you, "Do you work here in the office or out in the community?", don't be afraid to say, "Both." Yes, you are a teacher, or a health worker, or business advisor, but you are above all else a Peace Corps Volunteer. Also, feel free to write out a weekly work schedule that you can put on your desk. It will make it easier for everyone when they know where you are when you're out of the office.

- Remember the three goals of Peace Corps. How many have the word "job" in it? The second and third goals are not skills-focused, they're relationship-based. Make time in your work schedule to do this important work.

"Your work is going to fill a large part of your life, and the only way to be truly satisfied is to do what you believe is great work. And the only way to do great work is to love what you do. If you haven't found it yet, keep looking. Don't settle."
STEVE JOBS

Saying Hello

"Smiling and saying hi is probably one of the most important things," writes PCV Scott, *"especially in a small town."*

"If you want anyone to trust you, it's definitely going to help for you to get out of your house and start making friends. Even if your goal for that day is I'm going to make a new friend today and I'm going to walk out of my house, I'm going to find someone, I'm going to follow them around and learn what they do and talk to them. Make sure to work with the kids because they have all the time in the world for you."—PCV Amy

"To make the most of my Peace Corps experience in a small village of 1,000 people on the edge of the Gobi Desert, it was vital to be an integral part of the community, but that is easier said than done," says PCV James. *"The community consisted of many spheres of interaction: the faculty at school, my host family and relatives, students I instructed, and friends outside my workplace. It is ideal to penetrate through all these spheres of interaction to maximize the Peace Corps experience."*

PCV Leslie shares a story about just how big a small interaction can be: *"One summer, a young Mongolian girl just eight years old was resting on her windowsill enjoying the summer breeze when she looked onto the street and saw an American walking by. She waved her hand and yelled, "Hello!" to the Volunteer, the only word she knew in English. The Peace Corps Volunteer stopped walking and turned to smile at the girl, waved back and said, "Hello!" That was all that happened and all that was needed. She said right then and there, she decided she would do whatever she had to do to learn English and it changed her life forever. After years of learning English and going on to finish college, we met Tuul this summer during training. Fifteen summers later, she was now teaching our newest group of Peace Corps Volunteers how to speak Mongolian."*

It's a beautiful story about how Peace Corps works, how many years it can take to begin to understand their impact, and how important every moment of service is. All around the world, Peace Corps Volunteers hear "Hello!" in their communities, and it's nice to remember just how important one little hello was to one special girl.

Making Repairs

Take advantage of the early energy that comes with settling into your new home. The fresh eyes you have seeing your work, your community, and your new living space are priceless. Write a lot down now before you forget. Keep the excitement you have for as long as possible, and be careful of outside sources that might discourage you, such as community members or even other Peace Corps Volunteers. It is good to be realistic, but just because something hasn't been done before or has been like this for a long time doesn't mean it can't change, or that you can't be the source of that change. This could mean fixing up your place by making some simple home repairs, or suggesting ways to improve garbage collection around your building, or even suggesting a more effective strategy for meetings in your workplace. Even small changes can help make your service a lot more interesting.

"When I arrived in my new apartment, my bathroom faucet really needed replacing," writes PCV Travis. *"When my hospital handyman arrived he took the old faucet off, water still running in the pipes, and tried putting on the new one. Thirty minutes and buckets of water later, I realized just how handy I would need to become during my service."*

The repairs you want to make to your new home might seem overwhelming at first, but being in Peace Corps is a great place to learn a tremendous amount about handiwork such as fixing plumbing and electricity (if you have it), or taking up skills such as carpentry and repairing electronics. In America, we leave most repair work to professionals, but in most Peace Corps countries professionals are often hard to come by and "handymen" are around every corner. Learn from them, befriend them, and then do what they do—or maybe even improve upon their methods.

Improving Yourself

Perspective is very valuable during Peace Corps service. This includes perspective on your professional and personal self. As we've mentioned before, Peace Corps is fond of saying "you're on the job 24/7 as a Volunteer" and that comes with the added pressure of having to decide for yourself when you will work and when you will play. It's likely, for instance, that everyone you work with will start work in the morning and end in the evening. While they clock in and out of the office once, you might feel like you do so several times in one day. You might have a class or two here, a project or two there, and several meetings thrown in between. Then, when you go home from work, you write something that will eventually make its way to your American friends and family, through your blog, a letter, or conversation. It might not feel like it, but that's part of your job, too.

While changing the world, be sure to take some time for yourself. Remember when you take time for yourself you are offering a greater gift to the community. The old saying that you can't give what you don't have is true, whether you are referring to energy, wisdom, or even peanut butter. It takes time to get all of them, especially if you are starting from scratch. Give yourself the time and space to exercise, eat well, read, study, play, and enjoy your life. If you really are on the job 24/7, consider taking care of yourself part of your job. Schedule it in (if you are still using a schedule) and make sure to show up on time. Everyone will be glad you did when you are able to share your energy, wisdom, and even peanut butter. Who doesn't like homemade peanut butter?

*"To straighten the crooked you must first do a harder thing—
straighten yourself."*
BUDDHA

Always Changing

Peace Corps presents all of us with a tremendous amount of things that teach us that there is very little we can control. On any given day, you may be moved out of your apartment with no notice. You may be told to go here or there, or do this or that, and there is nothing you can do about it. You are in a society with its own rules—its own culture, way of thinking, and way of acting. In Peace Corps, it can feel like the rug gets pulled right out from underneath you so many times you start to lose count of how many rugs there must be. If you ask yourself, "What can I control?" you might be surprised by the answer. It isn't how other people act, or what happens or doesn't happen. The fact is, you might be moved to a new apartment, new job, or new project as soon as you finish this sentence. There could be a knock at your door and that is that.

What you *can* control is how you think and how you act. Try to take in all of the information around you, accept the reality of the situation you are faced with, and then choose how you are going to respond. Standing by your principles, especially in uncomfortable and difficult times, is a huge testament of your character. It's often when everything seems to fall apart and we are faced with challenge after challenge that we show what we are truly capable of. In fact, this seems to be a common element in all the happiest Volunteers we have come across. They aren't in perfect or comfortable situations; they have just decided to accept what is and to do the best they can with what they have.

*"The ultimate measure of a man is not where he stands in
moments of comfort and convenience, but where he stands at
times of challenge and controversy."*
MARTIN LUTHER KING, JR.

Cutting Out Middle Work

Busy work is often needlessly repetitive. Get good at cutting this out of the equation and just enjoy the good stuff. Take writing this handbook as an example: the words you are reading right now could have once been written on a napkin, then scribbled onto paper, then carefully and clearly rewritten on paper, then transcribed onto a computer, then edited and formatted to this page. If they had gone through all of these steps, this handbook would have taken six times longer to write, at least. Instead, we began with the end in mind, knew what the final product would look like, and skipped right to that. It saved us a lot of time and effort.

As you get involved in projects, conversations, and efforts in general, try to keep the end in mind and think about how to cut out the middle work if you can. There is no sense in writing on napkins if you don't have to, or in talking to 15 people when you are just delaying talking to the one person who you really need to talk to. Be realistic and long-range in your thinking; examine what the final outcome needs to be and the most effective way of getting there. Then, spend your extra free time earned doing stuff you really love.

> *"The shortest answer is doing the thing."*
> ERNEST HEMINGWAY

What's the Problem?

During training, one of the exercises they might put you through is the community and the problem. In this exercise, there are two groups: one is a group of community members and the other is a group of helpers from outside the community who have been told there is a problem. The helper group is also encouraged to be culturally sensitive. As the two groups meet for the first time, the real problem starts to unfold. The helpers come in asking questions and never get any satisfactory answers. They get confused, frustrated, and disappointed. The helpers usually end up thinking the community doesn't want to talk about their problem and the two groups feel separated by some invisible force. The separation, which isn't fully understood until the end when the facilitators explain it, exists because the community members were never told there was a problem. As far as they knew, everything was fine.

It's a fun and frustrating exercise and a powerful example of what Peace Corps is like. Very often, Peace Corps Volunteers may think they have identified a problem in the community, but later come to realize that they are the only ones who see it that way. As Carl Jung was famous for saying, "*When you have a hammer in your hand, every problem seems like a nail.*" It might take some getting used to, but you will probably get pretty good at putting down your hammer during Peace Corps service.

> "*As he simplifies his life, the laws of the universe will appear less complex, and solitude will not be solitude, nor poverty poverty, nor weakness weakness.*"
>
> HENRY DAVID THOREAU

Difficult Site Mates

"*Even though you might not have the best site mates, try to keep things as manageable as possible,*" says PCV Mary. "*If for some reason site mates do not work out, remember the other resources that you may have: texting other volunteers you are close with, spending more time getting to know people in your community and building those relationships, and talking with peer support if your post has it.*"

We are all in this together, but like any organization, some people will get along together better than others and some might not get along well at all. "*Go into Peace Corps assuming you won't have site mates living really close to you,*" says Mary, "*Definitely be ready for that possibility. Then consider it an unexpected blessing if you have great ones.*" The likelihood that you will be alone in your village, the vision most people have of life in the Peace Corps, is pretty high. Be ready for that and, even if you have site mates close to you, be ready to make it on your own.

"Be aware of the impact that you and your site mates have on one another," writes PCV Bonnie. *"Some relationships can be based on collaborating on projects, inspiring one another personally, and having a lot of fun becoming part of their community together. Others can be built around complaining about work, watching the latest American show download, and commiserating. Choose which relationship you want."*

> *"Keep away from people who try to belittle your ambitions. S mall people always do that, but the really great ones make you feel that you, too, can become great."*
> MARK TWAIN

Don't Do It

If you aren't passionate about it, if you don't believe in it, if it really isn't that important to you in the big picture, don't do it. Plain and simple. And don't say you "have to" when you really mean, "I'm scared of what will happen if I don't…"

You should *really* be scared about what will happen if you *do*. You will waste your time and your life doing work that's unimportant. You will burn out. You will ask yourself, "What's the point?" and be unable to answer. You will, in short, fail to find and live out your life's purpose and highest ideals. You are greater than that. This is why you are here.

There are PCVs worldwide challenging the idea of the normal 9–5. They travel, collaborate, move outside their sector, work odd hours, are away from "site," and engage in activities of every shape and size. Your work hours are 24/day; your "site" isn't your town, province, or even country—it's the entire world. Your colleagues sit next to you, and also at the edge of an e-mail and the end of a Skype webcam feed. Collaboration can bring you together with other sectors as easily as other countries. Engage because you love it, because you can't help yourself. If you think you have to do something you don't believe in, don't. Think again. Speak your mind and do what you love instead.

> *"Never confuse movement with action."*
> ERNEST HEMINGWAY

Have A Way Out

Here's a common situation: you're in a meeting, or sitting listening to something, and it's gotten to that point—it's irrelevant. You have to be there but you need a way out mentally. Here are two ideas for things you can do anytime or place when you have that spare minute (or hour):

Writing

Paper and pen are things you can always bring along with you and Peace Corps can provide great time and space to write. Maybe you have a book you've always wanted to publish, or a story you've wanted to record, or a few ideas you would like to share. Our advice, as you can see from the handbook you are holding, is to scribble down anything and everything that is meaningful to you and then collect it somewhere. Maybe in a journal, a folder, a series of Word documents, a quiver of blog entries, or chapters in your future paperback. Writing can be a very powerful way to collect your thoughts, share them with others, and maybe learn a thing or two about yourself.

Share Random Lessons

The combination of wonder, fear, excitement, frustration, newness, and humor in what you are experiencing during Peace Corps can sometimes be written in T9 text-message form. Title your random lessons of the day something catchy and send them to your Volunteer friends anytime something crazy or noteworthy happens. A few hundred messages later, you might find, like we did, that there is something very fun and cathartic to it.

Dream Awake

When someone says they're "living the dream" and they mean it, they've learned to do something that few people think is possible and even fewer actually do. They have learned to explore, define, and then act on their dreams. It could mean buying weights and finally getting into the best shape of your life, taking up hobbies that you've always secretly wanted to start, or pursuing an interest and love regardless of what kind of wealth or fame it may bring. Happiness is the ultimate currency; the thing that everyone wants and no one else can give you.

We can all become better. We can do a better job of living up to our ideals, living out our beliefs, and being the kind of people we want other people to be. We are already capable of it; we have everything we need to do it. It involves taking a breath, listening to something deep inside us, what we believe is most important in life, and then acting on that. It could be an idea you've always been afraid to turn into a reality, a dream that won't go away, or maybe a feeling that what you spend most of your day doing just isn't that important.

Love and live without fear, live in your dreams awake, simplify your life to only doing what you really believe is valuable. If you believe that serving other people is important, make that a priority in your job. Change your perspective. If you believe that kindness and love are important, be more helpful and give more easily. If you believe that integrity is valuable, be honest about who you are and what you think, especially when it's difficult.

"Our truest life is when we are in dreams awake."
HENRY DAVID THOREAU

Perfect Attendance

Peace Corps, and life in general, is not about punching a clock. There is a good old story of a doctor talking with a patient. The doctor asks, "How many hours a week do you work?" to which the man replies, "I don't know. How many hours a week do you breathe?" Work and the rest of our lives don't have to be separated, if we love what we do.

In fact, schedules in your host country probably don't matter as much as good work does. Instead of worrying about setting up a rigid schedule (which may fall apart anyway), concentrate on what good work you would like to do. Be open-minded to the likelihood that this will include working 4-hour days, 12-hour days, a weekend here and there, and several days "off" in between. At the end of your Peace Corps service it probably won't matter that you showed up to work at 9:00 AM and left at exactly 6:00 PM every day. The only thing that will matter is how meaningful your work was, how strong your relationships were, and how valuably you spent your time. Peace Corps is a 24/7 job as they say, but so is life. At the end of both you won't need to report perfect attendance; you will have an opportunity to show who you were and what you did. That will demonstrate whether you really ever showed up at all.

"When I finally let go of my idea of a schedule, I started making a much bigger impact in my own life and in the lives of those around me," writes PCV Bonnie. *"I don't know how many hours a day or a week I actually put in, but I'm confident that in the end, it all evens out as long as great projects and great relationships are happening."*

Making That Change

To be successful as a Peace Corps Volunteer, try to remember why you joined and what excited you, and continually find new reasons to stay and love it. A former Country Director once said, *"The happiest Volunteers are the ones who choose to be. They make a decision to be happy and find ways to do that."*

It's a powerful message, one that has been shared for generations (more recently by the likes of Michael Jackson, Mahatma Gandhi, John Lennon, and Barack Obama, to name a few). Listen to whatever it takes to encourage you to make that change you wish to see in the world around you. The happiest Peace Corps Volunteers are the ones who make peace with their situation and do everything they can with what they have. If you want a place to be more peaceful, be more peaceful yourself. If you want it to be better, be better yourself—be kinder and be stronger. *"What is the job of a PCV?"* wrote another Country Director. *"To do what you can, where you are, with what you have."*

> *"Enthusiasm is one of the most powerful engines of success.*
> *When you do a thing, do it with all your might.*
> *Put your whole soul into it. Stamp it with your own personality.*
> *Be active, be energetic, be enthusiastic and faithful, and*
> *you will accomplish your object. Nothing great was ever*
> *achieved without enthusiasm."*
> RALPH WALDO EMERSON

Projects

"One night we were hanging out with some Marines," writes PCV Jeff, *"who were at the part of their stint where they had to do a community project. One lamented that a $500 grant was impossible to work with. My reply? 'When the job's too tough for the Marines, they call in the Peace Corps'...then I ran."*

Projects can be a big, challenging, rewarding, frustrating, wonderful, and ridiculous part of your Peace Corps experience. Surprisingly, this can all seem to happen at the same time.

Try to keep in mind throughout the process that your old ideas of success might not apply in your new environment. In America, success usually includes efficiency, physical creation, and numbers on a page. However, in Peace Corps, success often includes a personal approach that is hard to quantify. Be confident as you begin to realize this could mean working to improve the quality of people's lives, the potential they see in themselves, and the opportunities that lie hidden within each of us. When Peace Corps Volunteers return to their host countries years later, people usually talk about very personal things they remember about the Volunteers: the way they lived, the way they inspired others, and the lessons they taught them. People change from the inside out and that often requires a lot less than a $500 grant.

> *"The person who says something is impossible should not interrupt the person who is doing it."*
> CHINESE PROVERB

Simplicity

You will often face situations during your Peace Corps service that seem very inconvenient, especially when you hold them up to American standards. We have lots of machines that replace human effort: conveyor belts, washing machines, dishwashers, vehicles, and construction equipment just to name a few. It can seem frustrating at first to do so many things by hand or to spend a lot of time doing something that you have seen done much faster by machines, but there are benefits to doing things more slowly. Are these actions—working, washing, walking, digging, moving, building, sharing, and working together with others—helping you to become a better person? Are you connecting at a deeper level with others, and with yourself? Things might not be more convenient, but maybe they are teaching us something we might never learn otherwise.

Generally speaking, Peace Corps slows down our fast-paced lives. Sometimes it even takes us back in time and gives us a chance to see civilization again for the first time. If you get a chance to slow down during your service, take the time to not mistake noise for wisdom, efficiency for value, or convenience for necessity. Some of the greatest lessons and interactions in your life are happening right now and they can take many forms. No matter when or where they come from, we hope you have plenty of time to really appreciate and enjoy them.

"Simplicity, simplicity, simplicity!" wrote Thoreau in Walden. *"I say let your affairs be as two or three, and not a hundred or a thousand; instead of a million count half a dozen…In the midst of this chopping sea of civilized life, such are the clouds and storms and quicksands and the thousand-and-one items to be allowed for, that a man has to live, if he would not founder and go to the bottom and not make his port at all, by dead reckoning, and he must be a great calculator indeed who succeeds. Simplify, Simplify."* And that was over 100 years ago!

Fitness

Take this time in Peace Corps to get into the best shape of your life. You will have the time; all you need is the motivation and the discipline to make it happen. Eat better, exercise more, and become that person you always wanted to be. Getting ripped could be easier than you think. Here are some thoughts from PCV James…

"Commitment to working out at least 20 minutes and stretching 10 minutes every day is key. That's what I did every morning, stretched first and then a set of push-ups and sit-ups. You don't need to do more than one set if you push yourself all out. Later in the day, you can do another set of push-ups and sit-ups if you want, but it's not really necessary (curls are fine, too.) Then I would rest on Saturday. On Sundays, I got up to doing 500 push-ups. It didn't matter how many repetitions or sets I did as long as there were 500 done before bedtime. Also, increase those reps. Let's say I did 50 push-ups today and I struggled. I'd stay on 50 for a couple of days. Then I'd move up to 52 the next time. Never go back down. That's how I reached 100 total in 1 rep after about 2 months."

We can vouch for James and how effective push-ups were for him, but you can make anything work for you if you stay consistent at it. Whether you like yoga, jogging, sports, lifting weights, or taking long walks, just stay at it. Get friends and other Volunteers to keep you accountable. They'll probably come along for the ride if you ask them.

How to Survive Vacation

Getting home to America for a vacation can be nice, but it can also be rough. Peace Corps's guide "On The Home Front" has some helpful information for your friends and family, but the best thing for them could be a couple conversations with you before you return home. Talk to your close friends about the things you've learned being overseas, how you feel about coming back to America, and challenges you anticipate having with the culture (American culture) and the people. It will be wonderful in so many ways, but don't get frustrated when it seems like you are crazy or you just don't feel like yourself. You will have changed some after being in another country for some time as well as living the life of a Peace Corps Volunteer, but that change has been for the better. Your friends and family will be surprised by this "new" you, but chances are they will appreciate the new light you shed on old experiences. Refresh yourself as well as those around you by just being yourself. If worst comes to worst, pretend your stomach is still adjusting to American food and sit in the bathroom for a while to get yourself together. (On second thought, you probably *won't* have to pretend.)

You will see a lot of things that are the same as when you left (consumerism, commercialism, and materialism), but it is likely that these things will be much more apparent to you than they ever were before. In your host country, the distance between the stuff you consume and the people who made it is likely very short. You know the woman who baked your bread, or the man who raised the goat that you ate; maybe you even killed the goat yourself. In America, the prices are high for the things we buy, and they're expensive. This will be a challenge. Try to be sensitive to the things you learned and loved in your Peace Corps experience.

Another challenge will be dealing with your family and friends with all of the newfound knowledge that you have about your world and yourself. Be patient with yourself, and with your family and friends. Take time to be alone and relax, and to collect your thoughts. Identify which of your friends are the best listeners and the most supportive, and share your concerns and thoughts with them. Tell them you don't need answers, exactly; you just want to share things with them. They might not know exactly what you are going through, but they will try to understand. This can make a world of difference.

Spend some time talking with other Peace Corps Volunteers. Talk with your friends back in your host country, or incoming or returned PCVs. Not only will they love to talk to you, but also they will be very understanding and supportive of what you are going through. You might feel a little crazy at times, or tired, or disappointed, or overwhelmed, but PCVs understand. They will be able to not only empathize with you but probably give you a few reasons to smile and laugh as well. Sometimes we get so deep in the forest that we can't see it for all the trees, as the saying goes. Taking a step back and talking with someone who knows what you are going through can help you remember where you are and why you are there.

Write down your experiences and thoughts, or turn them into music, poetry, paintings, sculptures, or art of any kind. However you like to release your thoughts and emotions, do that. It will help you sort through your experiences and make them a little more manageable. For instance, keep a list of all the things that are freaking you out about America. Every time something happens that freaks you out, write it down. Free toilet paper. Everybody talking in English. Six dollar coffee at Starbucks. Whatever it is, keep track of it. An overwhelming feeling then turns into a list, or a song, or a poem, and then it not only becomes manageable, it probably becomes pretty funny.

Sweeping

"Talking with a friend of mine who teaches in a Buddhist center is always an occasion for lots of laughs and great thoughts," writes PCV Travis. *"One of my favorite stories that he shared with me was about when he served in a monastery and was sweeping up one of the main*

assembly halls. As he was doing this one of the lamas, or oldest teach-ers, came in and said, 'Jim, why aren't you smiling or enjoying what you are doing?' then he leaned in as if telling him a secret and whis-pered, 'You know, it's going to be dirty again tomorrow.' Jim laughed and laughed as he repeated what the lama had said to him years ago. I love it. Jim has come a long way since then and I can see it in how much he enjoys everything he does, no matter what it is. I think this is a great lesson for anyone, but maybe especially for us as Peace Corps Volunteers."

Truly enjoying your life usually doesn't involve wishing for some other moment to replace this one or trying to fit as many things into this moment as possible. It involves being present, appreciating where you are, and making the most of it. Often it's not the end that we need to enjoy; it's all the small moments that make up our lives. Enjoy where you are, what you have, who you are with, and all of the other reasons why "right where you are" is one of the greatest moments of your life.

And remember, you probably missed a spot.

Let's Talk About This Last Year

Take some time with one of your close Peace Corps friends or one of your close friends from home and reflect on your previous year of service. You have many things to be proud of, many things to be excited about, and a couple things you probably want to improve upon. Talk these things out and, however you work through them best, record them and start to make out a work plan that helps you make your last year into an incredible year.

Keep in mind that it is often better to think about good rather than bad, positive rather than negative, and what you want to have happen rather than what you would rather not have happen.

You *could* worry about responsibilities, others' expectations, and how things will or won't work out. Or, you could spend your time on new ideas and projects, dreaming even bigger, and expect that things will go even better than you can hope if you really dedicate yourself to meaningful work. Less is often more, and when you apply that to your life (projects, websites, plans, daily activities, obligations) you can begin to focus on what is truly valuable and just let the rest slide.

As you think about this upcoming year, keep your options in mind for the years ahead, including extending for a third year of service at your current post (or maybe another Peace Corps post), serving with Peace Corps Response, applying for Peace Corps staff positions, or starting your applications for graduate school programs. Talk to your fellow Volunteers and Peace Corps staff to learn more about scholarship opportunities like Peace Corps Fellows/USA, and check out the resources on our website (travishellstrom.com/handbook), like the very informative Graduate School Guide written by Peace Corps. You have a world of options open to you; it might be hard to pick just one!

One More Year

At the one-year mark, your co-workers will likely take notice that you have one year of service left. They may want to know what you have done this past year, what you are doing now, and whether you can do more work with them. It is a great time to gather enthusiasm and choose the best projects and partners to work with. Writing out a work plan again can be very helpful, especially if you map out all of your remaining months of service, and what you plan to accomplish. Once you see the month of your Close of Service (COS) conference and the last month you will work, it really brings the reality home.

You have a set amount of time to finish projects, organize seminars, submit proposals for funding, and so on. Be realistic about the dates you set for starting and completing projects, but also be optimistic. Do the things you love and that excite you. Don't feel pressured by someone to accomplish new projects just because they tell you to. You work with your organization, but you work *for* Peace Corps. You have dedicated yourself to your community as a whole, to complete the projects that seem most helpful, achievable, and sustainable. Be respectful about considering new projects and possibilities during this upcoming year, but figure them into the bigger picture. Look at your work plan, month by month, and decide how new things might fit into the mix.

Lastly, surround yourself with your most enthusiastic and hardest working counterparts. They have been with you for a year, patiently listening to you and working with you. This is the year for you to really work best together and get things done. Honor their commitment to you by honoring your commitment to them. Be a good friend; be patient with them and listen to what they hope to accomplish with you in your last year. Oh yeah, and have fun!

What People Are Really Telling You

"Don't take things personally," writes PCV Mark. *"Lots of people get weird and say or do things that would normally offend you. Just let it slide, man. It's all part of the process."*

Almost 85 percent of the time (yes, we made that up), when speaking with someone, they aren't telling you anything about you; they are telling you about *themselves*. They are telling you about how they see the world—what is good, what is bad, who is good, who is bad, and on and on. This can be especially confusing when we aren't sure what we believe ourselves.

"After my first year of service, I met with one of my supervisors and she was very dissatisfied with my work. It was a difficult meeting and I took it very personally," writes PCV Travis. *"After a few days, however, I came to find out that our department was being pressured by the government and that that supervisor had similar meetings with just about everyone. A few weeks later, things were great again; it was crazy."*

When in doubt, a good tactic is to stay so busy being a good Volunteer that you don't have time to worry about whether people think you are one or aren't one. Take in information, whether it is "positive feedback" or "negative feedback," and examine how much truth it contains. If it is good information—*factual* information—

use it to improve your methods. If it is just opinion, feel free to let it go. A lot of the time, people bring more baggage to a situation than help. Relax and remember that everyone is trying to make sense of the world around them and do their best, sometimes we just disagree. We can respect one another, work together, and still hold differing views.

"What I must do is all that concerns me, not what the people think. This rule, equally arduous in actual and in intellectual life, may serve for the whole distinction between greatness and meanness."
RALPH WALDO EMERSON

Volunteers Together

After a year of service, it can be easy to forget the fact that the Volunteers you serve with are incredible and unique people. Rumors can fly. Relationships can change. Interactions can strain. It will be especially hard at times, but try to remember the greatness and potential that each of these people has within them. The things that you sacrifice to become a Volunteer, the daily struggles that you face, the projects and challenges and amazing experiences you go through are all things that many people never think they would be capable of doing, much less actually try. There is a very real reason why people say, "I could never do that," when you tell them about Peace Corps. Every day, you and your fellow Volunteers are doing things that many people simply can't do. Don't lose sight of that. Just like there is no such thing as a perfect Volunteer, there is no such thing as a *solo* Volunteer. We all have each other. The physical distance between us can't compare to the closeness that each of us can feel to each other just by being Volunteers together. We are part of an incredible group of caring, patient, and kind people who are far away from home trying to help others.

What Do You Do When Nothing Seems To Be Going Right?

Your counterparts aren't very interested in your even being alive. You don't seem to have anything remotely productive to do. Peace Corps is asking you to turn in a progress report and you are tempted to write, "Nothing to report." Is this what you signed up for? When Peace Corps said they were looking for "self-starters," did they mean "superhumans"? Well, yes and no. You signed up for a blank slate, a place for you to make your mark, however you wish. And no, you don't need to be superhuman, just human. In fact, in our opinion, being human is probably one of the most "productive" things you can do during your service.

Coming from America, the land of plenty (of work, money, entertainment, success, and other arguably important things), it is normal to be frustrated by what might appear to be a lack of initiative, confusion, bureaucracy, and ineffectiveness in your host country agency. It's not only understandable, it's awesome that you are motivated to do good work, even *great* work. With that being said, we're sorry to say that there is no secret here. There's no magic bullet. We've been there and we've learned a few things, but one of the biggest things we've learned is that this challenge is present in every Peace Corps country in every corner of the world. You're not alone and you're not a bad Volunteer. We are right here with you. We're aren't going to tell you to "suck it up" or "think more positively" or any other ridiculously simple advice. Like every other page in this handbook, we are just going to share a few things that helped us through these difficult periods. We hope they are helpful for you.

Talk to Your Fellow Volunteers

It can be very helpful to talk with fellow Volunteers in your country, both within your group and in groups that came before you. Volunteers within your group, though you might not know it, are often going through the same challenges you are. You can check out the 27-Month Cycle in the Resources section at the back of this handbook to see a general overview of how things might be going. Also, as you might imagine, talking with Volunteers in groups that came to your host country before you can be very helpful, offering you some future perspective on the situation. Their understanding and support can often be surprising and exact.

A word of caution: don't necessarily talk with the Volunteers you feel closest too, especially if you think they might compound on the negativity. Seek out Volunteers who can be realistic but also optimistic about the situation, who can listen without necessarily telling you what to do and who are role models themselves. In short, talk to people who are as you would like to be.

Talk To Volunteers in Other Places

As before, we found it helpful to not only talk with Volunteers in our country, but also ones outside our country. It's kind of amazing how much we all have in common, whether we are in a mud hut or an apartment, experiencing scorching hot sun or Siberian winters. *"During one of the low points in my service,"* writes PCV Mary, *"I spoke with a friend who was serving in another country. He was having the same exact problems with his deputy director that I was having with mine! He felt just as depressed as I did, and here I was thinking that everything was going so well for him."* Especially after Peace Corps, many Volunteers comment on how there is a special bond between fellow RPCVs from around the world that they can't quite explain. That bond can start during service as well.

Focus on Individuals

It's easy to get trapped in a utilitarian mindset, where you want to do the greatest good for the greatest number of people. In Peace Corps, many days, the greatest number is one. The person right in front of you, the counterpart who can't speak much English, the student who is having trouble, the businesswoman who is trying to make things work—they could all use your help, even if they can't tell you that clearly. Ask their name. Remember it. Get to know them a little before asking them how you can help them. What is their family like? What do they like to do inside and outside of work? What is most important to them in their life? If you ask questions the right way or if you are really listening and giving yourself fully to understanding them, you might be surprised by what you learn. It's our opinion that fancy words like "capacity building" and "sustainable development" confuse the fact that we are really talking about relationships. Friendship. Real people. Be a good friend and you'll listen, you'll understand, and you'll offer to help. Be a good Volunteer and you'll do the same. Listen. Understand. Help. Remember, this takes more than an afternoon. The listening part, as you know from trying to learn a new language, can take months. Understanding can take many more months and in fact, spending your whole first year as a Volunteer trying to understanding isn't a bad idea. As for the helping part, that can vary; just smiling, patting someone on the shoulder, laughing, sharing your snacks, and opening the door for someone helps them in small ways. The bigger things, like projects, seminars, and so forth, can build from there. It can be a wonderful thing that, during Peace Corps, you begin to blur the line between personal and professional relationships. Most countries don't see it the way America does, where we are one person in the office and another person outside it, which explains why coworkers sometimes go into the countryside during the workweek to help comb sheep's wool in the spring. Being a good Volunteer and being a good friend can often involve doing the exact same thing.

Do Great Work

There is difference between good work and great work. Good work is productive, like editing a spreadsheet and holding meetings to brainstorm and get everyone up to speed. Great work is revolutionary, like the ideas that wake you up at night because you are so excited about them. Passion, innovation, enthusiasm, and vision thrive in great work.

Jumping Out of the Box

Years ago, a doctor conducted a series of experiments with groups of dogs. One group of dogs was given electric shocks, but could stop them by touching their nose to a panel. A second group was given the shocks also, but had no way to stop them. The dogs in the first group recovered well from the experiment, but the dogs in the second group, those that had been helpless, developed symptoms similar to clinical depression.

In the second half of the experiment, the dogs were placed in a box with a low barrier. When the shocks were given, all the dogs could escape the pain by jumping out, and this is what the dogs from the first group did. But the dogs from the second group just lay there whimpering. The researcher, Dr. Seligman, called this "learned helplessness." The experiment was repeated with other animals, and even humans, but the results were always the same. Once the subjects had been in a situation over which they had no control, most continued to feel helpless, even in situations where they *did* have control.

However, some subjects, about a third, were able to endure the difficulty and still not develop "learned helplessness." Instead, they bounced back and were stronger. Dr. Seligman called this "explanatory style," the way we explain things in our lives. He found that those who bounced back chose ideas like "not me, not always, not everything" to explain their experience rather than "me, always, everything." This can apply profoundly to each of our lives.

When something bad happens—and plenty of bad things happen in Peace Corps—it's tempting to think it's our fault and it will always be this way. But that's rarely true. We are making a choice, just like the subjects inside the box, to stay in our current belief system regardless of the pain it causes us. If you have the chance to jump out of your old pattern of thinking, even for a moment, we say go for it.

Value > Efficiency

Americans are often very efficient people, scheduling our lives down to the minute. Efficiency can be nice, but often our Peace Corps host countries put a lot more focus on value. Trying to be a valuable person and being involved in valuable work can make your service in Peace Corps reach another level of helpfulness to the people around you.

In Peace Corps, we have a unique opportunity to revisit our life schedules and compare them to new opportunities and dreams. If you can't categorize exactly where you are going or what you will do, just keep thinking about your passions and what you love. Write them down, share them with friends and family, and ask for help with funding, planning, or fulfilling your dreams. It will probably work. You could go places you never planned, become more skilled in diverse fields, complete successful projects, get into the best shape of your life, and have tons of fun. The more dreams you share, the easier it will be to think of bigger and crazier ones. The old idea—that if you love what you do, you will never work a day in your life—can become reality. Maybe you could live the rest of your life doing things you love and not worry about work. Your dreams probably aren't that crazy after all; maybe they involve simple pleasures like learning guitar or becoming a better cook, helping people around the world or writing a book. When people say follow your bliss, listen to your passions, live the life you've dreamed of, maybe you will be the person they think of.

Ask yourself why you are doing what you are doing, what outcome you are hoping to achieve, and how that measures up to other ways you could spend your time. When you get to the end of your service, you will probably remember the relationships you formed, the projects you loved, and the dreams you achieved. Focus on the things you love and, efficient or not, you will do a lot of good work.

Serving Your Passion

Why do you do what you do? If you feel called to certain projects, activities, or people more than others, don't feel bad about giving yourself to serving those things. The extra energy you bring to your passions is worth its weight in gold. You will inspire others, stay motivated longer, and feel like you aren't working at all…you're just doing what you love.

Peace Corps Volunteers are usually very passionate people, people who love what they do. During your service, it might be helpful for you to take time to sit back and reflect on questions that inspire you to rediscover or recommit yourself to the things that are most important in your life. On the next few pages, we have included some thoughts on passion that were helpful for us. We hope they are helpful for you, too.

If you'd like to go even deeper, visit travishellstrom.com/purpose to find a four-part video series on *Crafting Your Purpose*.

> *"Choose a job you love and you'll never have to work a day in your life."*
> Confucius

What are you good at?

From elementary school all the way to the present moment, where have your talents been, where do you naturally excel, when do people ask you for advice and help? You might not think of these things regularly; you just do them really well. Think about your hobbies, skills, relationships, responsibilities, past work, projects, honors, and awards. Have you always been a good writer, speaker, artist, organizer, builder, teacher, or friend? Have you been good at ideas, connecting people, leading, gardening, or selling things? Give this some thought; often we forget about what we do well.

What excites you?

This may be something you do regularly or something you would do all the time if you could. When you talk about these things, you light up. In a bookstore, what sections do you go to first and easily forget how long you've been there? What do you read online for hours in multiple tabs or talk to friends about until the sun comes up? It could be something you haven't done in awhile.

> *"You can only become truly accomplished at something you love...*
> *Pursue the things you love doing, and then do them so well that*
> *people can't take their eyes off you."*
> MAYA ANGELOU

What have you secretly dreamed of?

You might have some ridiculous dream you've always wanted to achieve but some fear or self-doubt has held you back and led you to dismiss the idea. Maybe there are several. No matter what doubt you might have about achieving it, or how unrealistic it might seem, what would you attempt to do if you knew you wouldn't fail? Is there something you have always felt you should do with your life, even though you've ignored those thoughts in the past? Take as much time as you want on this question.

If you haven't thought over these questions in a while, you might be surprised by what you see. Passion can be hidden, but it always wants to surface. Look back over your answers and circle some of the things you would really consider your passions. Here are some suggestions, which you might like to try out during your Peace Corps service:

List... Make a list of things you want to learn, need to improve on, skills you want to master, and people you want to talk to.

Ask... Talk to people who have been successful in the field you're interested in (maybe in person, through their blogs, or via e-mail).

Experiment... If you haven't already, start to do the thing you've chosen. If you've already started, make it public however you can. This will motivate you to improve, gets you feedback, and your reputation will improve as you do.

Have No Fear... This is the biggest obstacle for most people: self-doubt and fear of failure. Acknowledge it rather than ignoring or denying it. Write it down, accept it, and ask yourself, "What's the worst that can happen?" Usually, it's not catastrophic. Prepare yourself for it, and then do it. Take small steps and forget about what might happen. Focus on what is actually happening, right now. And then celebrate your success with those closest to you.

Start with a Few... Don't take on too many passions at once, maybe three to five. Ask yourself which ones get you the most excited, which you'd love to share.

Find the Time... This shouldn't be too hard with the flexible schedule you have in Peace Corps, but make the time if you have to. Rearrange your life until you have the time. This might mean waking up earlier, or doing it after work or during lunch, or on weekends. It may mean canceling some commitments or simplifying your work routine. Do what it takes.

Make Money Doing It... You might be surprised to find that you can make money following your passion. Embrace this and use it for good around the world. While you can't make money as a Peace Corps Volunteer, you can fuel projects with your talents and connections. The very book you are holding in your hands is a perfect example of a passion (writing) that makes money and now funds Peace Corps projects around the world.

Be Surprised... Your passion is worth every second, every ounce of your courage and effort. It will transform your life, give you that reason to jump out of bed, and make you happy no matter how much you make.

Ask and You Shall Receive

It may surprise you at first, but every time you really want something and then share that with others, it will probably happen. Share your hopes and dreams with your friends and fellow Volunteers, which you previously kept to yourself, and then new doors may open that make achieving those dreams easier than you ever could have imagined. The more you walk down the path of being honest about what you think and want (whether it's spiritual growth, world peace, or exciting projects,) the more people will step out from the bushes and start walking with you.

This requires two key actions, which most people never put together. First, you have to be really sure of what you want. The more you reflect and meditate on what you believe to be most important, the more temporary pleasures and pains fade and permanent experiences remain. If you want things that are beyond yourself, this will be an important part of why other people will be so excited to help out. Second, share your thoughts with people very clearly and practically. If you know people have talents and interests in a certain area, ask for their guidance. If you think a certain company could sponsor an idea, send a request. Instead of just thinking about your dreams, start *acting* on them. Make documents and web pages outlining a plan of attack. Don't ask your inner fears for advice; ask people you admire and trust. Share dreams with several people to get a wider view on the possibilities. Sometimes what you think you need is only just the beginning of a longer and much more incredible journey than you could have understood at the start. More experienced people will probably be patient and unbelievably generous to you when you are honest and clear about your intentions. Be ready to get much more than you could ever expect.

"Not Wastes of Time"

You will run into lots of things that feel like wastes of time during your service. "*One helpful practice I began in my second year,*" writes PCV Travis, "*was writing down in a place I saw everyday at work a list of things that I had learned were not wastes of time. Not only did this list remind me of what to do when I was at work, but it also stopped me from doing other things that weren't on my list.*"

It can be frustrating to see people talk about things they don't act on. It solves the "problem" of not being busy, but there is plenty of busy-ness to go around: numbers for spaces, words for lines, paper for binders, and people for chairs. Saying "I'm busy" is not the same as "I am doing something of value." The second one is really tricky. Ultimately, it comes down to your view on life and purpose, existence, and happiness themselves. Figure out your ultimate answers to those big questions and then put your work into the equation. That's when value shows or doesn't.

The frustrating thing isn't so much that people waste their time as it is that we waste our own time. We talk, but fail to act. We read, but fail to take notes and apply lessons. We hear, but fail to listen. We have the ability to be great, but fail to utilize the opportunities before us. As the saying goes, the man who doesn't read has no advantage over the man who can't. Reading, talking, hoping, planning, preparing, researching, and discussing all need to precede action. Peace Corps can be a powerful time to relearn that lesson.

When it comes down to it, at the end of your Peace Corps service what you did that you are proud of will be the things that are on that list: helping counterparts who amaze you, working on those projects that get you up in the morning, and following that passion of yours that just won't go away. Everything else will likely be forgotten.

Greatness and Roots

You may find your frustration often lies not in what is happening, but in your own ability to react to it properly. This could mean your perspective or maybe your management of projects and activities. You want to be a kind and effective person, engaged in healthy and meaningful work. This requires avoiding the easy trap of doing what is urgent but not valuable, or immediate but not lasting.

Before Peace Corps, you may have carried around your planner all the time, always accompanying you so you would be on task. Maybe you were effective in large part because of the amount of time you put into planning, organizing, and prioritizing things. However, over the course of your service you may live in a culture that is much more lenient about time, which can be a great opportunity for you to learn about the differences between greatness and effectiveness.

If effectiveness is doing things right, greatness is doing the right things. It requires value judgment, vision, and having a clear idea of why you do what you do. It requires that you ask yourself what the ultimate reason is behind it all. How does purpose live out through doing this thing? It might seem unreasonable at first to ask yourself how buying this thing or filling out this form or finishing this project helps you live out your life's purpose, but you might find it is of utmost importance to consider it. PCV Travis shares the following story...

"One of the greatest things I've learned in Peace Corps has been that, between all of the pleasure and the pain, we are all after a deep happiness in life. We pursue it through our relationships, our professions, our projects, and most of all through our day-to-day interactions with the people we bump into. It's beautiful in a small town to see people helping each other and truly not leaving anyone out in the cold.

I have never heard of a homeless shelter, orphanage or retirement home in our province. They don't need them. People open their homes to their siblings, cousins, aunts and uncles, grandparents, and relatives year after year. It's very likely, in fact, that we five Peace Corps Volunteer are the only people living alone in this province of 50,000 people.

When speaking about my life in Peace Corps, I have often said to my friends and family that I spend most of my time just trying to be a good person. I try to treat every interaction, every choice, every moment, as a chance to make a good decision. This is a lot harder than I thought it would be. At first, I thought it meant showing up to work at exactly

9 AM and leaving at exactly 6 PM. It didn't. Then I thought it meant working really hard on projects and getting lots of money for proposals and seminars. That wasn't it, either. That was my efficient mind trying to quantify what I am going through. When my mind opened up to the idea of quality instead, the whole situation changed."

Henry David Thoreau once said, *"There are a thousand hacking at the branches of evil to one who is striking at the root."* The difference between an effective project and a great project, or an effective person and a great person, may just be the difference between branches and roots.

Generosity and Possession

Think about these words. Home. My home. Office. My office. Problem. My problem. Possession and the attachment it comes with can cause a lot of suffering if it isn't kept in perspective. Most Volunteers come into Peace Corps as very generous people, but the experience will push you even further with your generosity. In fact, you might come into a culture that blows you away with its generosity. In some cultures the words "I," "me," "my," and "mine" aren't really given much thought—certainly not as much thought as in America. Hold on past the frustration and fascination this can provide and get ready for the insight and the drop in ego it inspires. Whatever religious tradition you find yourself surrounded by in your host country and whatever religious tradition you bring with you, the golden rule is probably in there somewhere. The idea that we should treat others as we would have them treat us is a tall order. Compassion requires ultimate generosity and isn't for the faint of heart. Let loose of your grip on whatever view you came in with and open up your heart and mind to the possibility that your old ideas of generosity and possession need to become a little wider than before.

"We make ourselves rich by making our wants few...A man is rich in proportion to the things he can afford to let alone."
HENRY DAVID THOREAU

Guardian Angels

PCV Alex shares this wonderful story she was told by her mother: *"There are many people in the world who are not fortunate enough to help others because they themselves need help. One can only give what they have. Even though we ourselves aren't perfect and we don't have everything figured out just yet, we are fortunate enough to have some things that we can give. So why not give them out? The reason that a guardian angel is such a special person in one's life is because they are rare; one may go through life never meeting one. But think about how easy it is to be someone else's guardian angel. All you have to do is provide the knowledge or things that you already possess. And who knows, maybe the person you once helped may turn out to be yours."*

It's a beautiful concept and one that we can each employ in our lives, whether we are a teacher, a youth volunteer, a business advisor, a health worker, or a friend. Don't forget how important those individuals have been who have changed your life in the past, because that's exactly who you can be for someone else.

Somethings

Speaking a new language (or listening to a new language, which is more often what we do at first) teaches the power and uselessness of words like nothing else. You watch people talk and talk, and for what? Sometimes something. Sometimes nothing. Avoiding the nothings and placing just the right words in those moments of something is an art. The right words, even a single one, can do something that a thousand wrong words can't. Learning a new language gives one the chance to hear a thousand hollow words, but also if we are lucky we get to hear the right words, the words full of meaning—timeless, well-placed, helpful, kind, something words. It's not easy, and takes a lot of practice, but it can mean the world to people all around you. The right words can heal, lead, inspire, and change lives. And when the right words and deeds align, you have something else entirely, something that can change the world.

"Better than a thousand hollow words, is one word that brings peace."
BUDDHA

Definition of Success

"One of my most vivid memories of preparing to leave for Peace Corps was when our trainers asked us to open up our handbooks and write down our definitions of success as Peace Corps Volunteers," writes PCV Travis. *"I think we were given 5–10 minutes. I thought to myself then that I wanted more time. I wrote for as long as they let me and continued to write for two years. I still want more time."*

This might be the single most important question any Peace Corps Volunteer can ask themselves. What is success? How will you know you were successful? Your own answer takes time and it may take your heart, your service, and your whole life to write.

"Go to the people, live with the people. Learn from them, love them. Start with what they know. Build on what they have. But with the best leaders, when the work is done the people all say, We have done it ourselves.""
LAO TZU

MY NOTES

RETURNING TO AMERICA

COS Conference

COS, meaning both "close of service" and "continuation of service," hasn't always existed. It has evolved as Peace Corps has grown over the last 50 years, offering Volunteers support and resources to help with their transition from life as a PCV to life as an RPCV.

During the COS conference, you will receive a lot of interesting and valuable information—both person-to-person through panel discussions with RPCVs and sessions with your Peace Corps staff, as well as in print through great resources like the RPCV Handbook. We know a lot of COS involves paperwork and might seem like business as usual, but we hope it gives you a great chance to get together with your fellow Volunteers one last time, take those last group pictures, and walk away with the information you will need for the months ahead.

In this "Returning to America" section, we will be exploring some of the common challenges that face RPCVs and ways to meet those challenges. We will also be focusing more on your "continuation of service" rather than your "close of service," since resources like the RPCV Handbook (which we highly recommend) provides in-depth coverage of that information. As former Peace Corps Director Loret Miller Ruppe said, the job of a Peace Corps Volunteer is, *"to learn peace, to live peace and to labor for peace from the beginning of our service until the end of our lives."* We hope the following information is helpful for your next 27 months of service, and the 27 months after that...

Common Challenges

There are many challenges that RPCVs face soon after completing their service. Here are five common challenges shared by dozens of Volunteers, courtesy of Sara, who supports RPCVs returning home from their service. (You can find more about Sara in our Resources section.)

#1: A tendency to compare themselves to their peers who didn't serve, and have been busy building their careers and earning income while the RPCVs have been volunteering.

Many RPCVs express that they had higher academic (and potentially professional) achievement than many of their peers before service, but upon coming home, they often feel behind the curve when they see peers buying homes, getting married, having children, etc. This is complicated by the fact that many RPCVs stay with their parents immediately following service, where they often feel a lack of independence.

RPCVs also sometimes feel the value and skills developed in their Peace Corps experiences can be harder to articulate on resumes and in interviews than that of their peers, and the lack of financial resources can lead to feelings of inadequacy.

"My whole life I've had all the hallmarks of success—academic success, involved in community..." says one RPCV. "But when I came back from Peace Corps, I didn't have any money and was very jealous of my classmates with their outward success (homes, jobs, etc.). I felt fearful that I was now off track."

#2: Lack of clarity on what they'd like to do next, reluctance to commit to a job before they know what they want their next step to be, and fear that it won't be as fulfilling as their Peace Corps service.

Most RPCVs have a variety of interests, and through Peace Corps (and potentially prior experiences), many have also developed a deep passion for direct service: interaction with the community they are serving daily. They find, however, that a lot of the jobs with the populations/issues they are interested in serving are more administrative, and don't light them up the way their Peace Corps experiences did. Many RPCVs fear that even when they do select work, it won't have the same challenge, variety, depth, and fulfillment that their volunteer experiences had.

One RPCV expresses it this way: "I fear I'm not going to learn anything new. I'm going to get a job and become complacent and not challenge myself."

Some expressed that they thought they would only really be happy if they did freelance or entrepreneurial ventures, but felt they didn't have the start-up capital or knowledge to pull these off.

#3: Struggle to fit into their communities at home, and feeling a void without the communities they built in their host countries.

When newly home, many RPCVS feel that there are few who want to hear the whole story of their Peace Corps experiences, and sometimes the volunteers feel they have little else to talk about. As a result, some fear they have "nothing to add to friend conversations," and don't want to be that person who's always like, "Well, in *Peru*..." After living in much simpler cultures without as much Internet access, many also expressed feeling somewhat overwhelmed and isolated with technology: smart phone apps, new forms of social media, etc. Many say that they relate best to other RPCVs, who don't usually live in their home cities.

At the same time, many volunteers also find they deeply miss the communities they built in their host countries, which were a central part of their service. As one RPCV put it, "The most sustainable thing

I think volunteers really do is their relationships. In the end, you just want to be with those people; the work is secondary almost."

#4: Difficulty juggling their desire to connect with their families and other loved ones with work they may like to do in areas away from them.

After two years away, most RPCVs are naturally very enthusiastic about reconnecting with family and friends. They want quality time with these people, and many volunteers express that their parents (especially) feel joyful and relieved that they are home, and even if they don't say it outright, they would like them to stay close. This often conflicts with the type of work RPCVs find most intriguing—either in U.S. cities outside of their hometowns, or back abroad.

One RPCV, considering work in a refugee camp that really excites her, says, "I just got home. They say they'll support whatever I do, but I know it would be so hard for them. I can't do that to my parents."

#5: Fear that they were top versions of themselves during Peace Corps, and aren't sure they'll be able to be those people again.

Most RPCVs are very proud of their Peace Corps service and the way they successfully managed a whole host of language, cultural, and other challenges on a daily basis. As one RPCV expresses, the experience helped her feel impressed by herself, which led to confidence in various aspects of her life during service. "I would think: 'I just navigated *that*! There's no stopping me!'" When she got home, however, both that level of daily challenge and the confidence that came with coping with it was not readily available.

Another volunteer says, "I feel like I was the best version of myself during Peace Corps . . . and sometimes wonder if I'll be able to get back to that mental place." He says that, in particular, during Peace Corps, he felt like he well understood the values of "enough" (versus excess), and of not comparing himself to others. Being back in the States, though, he has found it much more difficult not to judge himself against his peers (as expressed in #1), and to have expectations for what he needs to be and do.

Connecting Together

If you haven't heard of it already, the National Peace Corps Association (NPCA) is the largest organization in the world supporting RPCVs. It is headquartered across the street from the national Peace Corps office in Washington, D.C. and works every day to support members and friends of the Peace Corps community. NPCA is a wonderful network of tens of thousands of Volunteers from around the world and a great place to get connected to people who know and love the Peace Corps.

Several of the topics in this section, including RPCV Mentoring, Bringing the World Home, and Speaking Out, were written with our friends at NPCA. They are a great group of people who care deeply about Peace Corps and Peace Corps Volunteers, and we hope you are able to connect together with them. Throughout your service as a Peace Corps Volunteer and for your first year as an RPCV, you have been given free membership in the NPCA and up to three other member organizations (like Friends of Malawi, Charlotte Area RPCVs, or Lesbian, Gay, Bisexual & Transgender RPCVs). We hope you enjoy these resources and the chance it gives you, as a member of the Peace Corps community, to connect with others and continue enjoying your Peace Corps experience. To learn more about NPCA check out their website at www.PeaceCorpsConnect.org.

RPCV Mentoring

Returning home from Peace Corps service is rarely an easy process. The thought of "What now?" is often a daunting one, and is frequently exacerbated by reverse culture shock that can be more difficult to navigate than the culture shock experienced at the start of one's service. What was once familiar now seems foreign, making it all the more challenging for a newly-returned Volunteer to re-establish himself or herself.

This situation is one with which nearly every RPCV can identify. However, today's Volunteers are returning to one of the harshest economical environments in decades, further complicating their transition. When considering these issues in relation to the "Bringing the World Home" goal, a significant question emerges: How can recently returned Volunteers bring the world home when they're having enough trouble getting though the process of simply coming home?

When your family and friends would rather discuss their favorite TV show than hear your stories, when no one understands why the cereal aisle gives you the shakes…we get it. Trust us. No matter where you served or when you served, your fellow RPCVs get it. You can be at a swanky party talking to some random person and somehow when Peace Corps is mentioned, *boom*, you have a new best friend. You don't really know anything about them; they don't really know anything about you. But because you have Peace Corps in common, you all of a sudden have this…connection.

In 2007, the National Peace Corps Association sought to create a more formalized system of support for newly COSed Volunteers. Through a cooperative agreement with Peace Corps, they launched the RPCV Mentoring Program. Today, the program has expanded to 35 participating NPCA member groups and nearly 1,000 mentors and mentees.

Although there are instances where there are no mentors located near a mentee and vice-versa, participants utilize both traditional and new communication media (such as Skype) to connect.

As mentee Anne Varnell says, *"I have only good things to say because I was very isolated and just having someone reach out to me even though they were not living in my area helped me through some very hard times. Though your loved ones want to help, having the ability to reach out to a RPCV mentor provides a safe environment to ask for guidance or to voice frustration, fear, and confusion."*

While there have been many successes in the RPCV Mentoring Program, there is always room for improvement. Recognizing this, NPCA launched a new mentoring site in the fall of 2010 that allows the matching process to become both easier and more user-driven. Mentees who register are able to search for a mentor themselves, and seek assistance from both NPCA and the participating member groups should they need help finding a match. The site also features a social networking space where mentors and mentees can share ideas and resources on a wide range of topics related to the mentoring process, including careers, education, networking, and transitional guidance. If you are interested in the RPCV Mentoring Program, please visit www.rpcvmentoring.org.

For the record, from the moment you're sworn in you're a Peace Corps Volunteer, and when you leave, you're an RPCV. Many Volunteers who end their service early for whatever reason often feel as though they are somehow not in the RPCV "club." Balderdash. RPCVs know that people terminate their service for all sorts of reasons —some voluntary, some involuntary. Don't sweat it. As long as you didn't do something totally egregious, we're happy to count you as one of us.

Unexpected

Not every Peace Corps Volunteer finishes their service when they initially planned on it. In fact, there are many circumstances (especially medical separations) which can come up unexpectedly. PCV Mike shares this story:

"I would imagine that everyone has a different experience coming home from service; mine was no exception. After serving a year in Mongolia with my wife, we were called to train the incoming class of Volunteers during the summer. It was a welcomed vacation from ger life (a "ger" is a traditional Mongolian felt tent) after a particularly brutal winter. We had every intention of finishing up our tour when the unexpected happened; the PCMO told my wife that she was pregnant and that we were going to be medical separated. We had 10 days to leave the country. When we arrived at our home, our host family had just finished putting up a new ger for our mother who was scheduled to visit from America in two weeks. It was heartbreaking to tell them that we had to leave; they were our best friends in Mongolia. We also had to quit our jobs, including my wife's school who loved her and tried to convince

her to just get an abortion so we could stay. We spent two days packing up and saying goodbye. It took about three days to complete our close of service stuff and we wrestled with the conflicting emotions of what was transpiring in our lives. It was like being trapped on a rollercoaster, we literally had no control over what was happening to us. All of a sudden, we were on a plane out of the country, Ulaanbaatar to Beijing, Beijing to Chicago. Boom. Now we are home. Home with no job, no place to live, no car, no plans, and a baby on the way. The fear was palpable.

However, we were PCVs (well, technically RPCVs at this point) and we could accomplish anything—the most important lesson I learned in the Peace Corps. We were fine, we ended up making it. And now we have a great souvenir of our time in Mongolia."

Reaching Out as You Finish Your Service

There are several things you can do to get ahead of the game at any time. These include putting yourself out there, connecting with mentors, and summarizing your service.

Putting Yourself Out There

Personal branding in the digital age is a hot topic, and there are several great resources out there (which we have included in the Resources section at the back of this handbook). Whether you want to create your own website (which you can do for free), put yourself up on LinkedIn, or just make your Facebook profile more professional, there are a lot of steps you can take now to prepare yourself for your next step. The reality of the digital world that we all live in is that you are on the internet, whether you like it or not. People are going to Google you, potential employers definitely included. Creating your own personal brand means proactively engaging with that reality, making sure that when people do look you up, you know (and hopefully like) what they are seeing. That's basically what SEO (search engine optimization) is, in a nutshell. Companies and individuals around the world are doing it, and if you want to be proactive, there are some great things you can do to get started:

Take a second look at your social media profiles:

- When someone looks for you online, chances are the first things that pop up will be your Facebook, Myspace, Twitter, or other social media profiles.
- If you want to make them professional, share things you are proud of and imagine yourself as a potential employer looking over them. Make sure you come across as the kind of person you want to.
- If you want to hide these profiles, go into your settings and set who can see what, whether they be pictures, journal entries, or comments on other pages.

Update your LinkedIn:

- LinkedIn was started as a professional social media website, connecting professionals (who can join for free) with organizations (who can pay to connect with them). It has maintained its reputation for being a place where people share their resumes, their official associations, and professional ambitions.
- By joining LinkedIn, you can connect with organizations you've worked for, upload information about your resume which potential employers can view easily online, and also ask for people to provide official recommendations for you.
- LinkedIn is also a great way to meet people through friends of friends. When you search for someone, say in a company you want to work for, LinkedIn will tell you if you are connected to them through someone else. Then you can ask your friend on LinkedIn to introduce you and start the conversation from there, which is much better than a cold call or an e-mail out of nowhere.

Create your own website for free:

- Starting your own website has never been easier. Using free sites like Google Sites, Weebly, or Tumblr, you can upload your resume or weekly thoughts and even buy your own domain name (like www.yourname.com) for as little as $7 a year. That's how this handbook's website was made (travishellstrom.com/handbook) and we'd be glad to walk you through the process. We promise it's much easier than you might think.

Connect with Mentors

Surprisingly, few people reach out to those they admire, whether they be famous authors, musicians, professionals, or supervisors. We can tell you that with confidence because we've been there. We've given those presentations that took weeks to prepare, and then had no one come up afterward to say thank you. You've probably been there too; maybe even today, right?

The point is, it's easier to connect with people than you think. Stay after class an extra minute to say thanks to the teacher. Write a short thank you note to the author of a book that you enjoyed. Send an e-mail or a message to someone who made your day. Connect online with people who would love to help you.

Whether you connect with PCV friends of yours (maybe in your group or from your host country), or RPCVs in the broader Peace Corps community who are excited to meet you (through RPCV groups of the RPCV Mentoring program), we will wager to guess that there are some great people out there who would love to help you out. Search on Facebook, or connect with the NPCA website or the RPCVMentoring.org project. We bet you will be surprised by how many awesome people are out there. Remember, you're only a stranger once.

Start Your Dos Anytime

Your Description of Service (DOS) is the official summary of your Peace Corps service. It's signed by your Country Director and also has a paragraph explaining your Non-Competitive Eligibility, which you will learn about at your Close of Service (COS) conference. What most Volunteers don't realize is that you can work on your

DOS at any time during your service and, like most things (such as resumes), it's often easier to work on it along the way rather than all at once at the end when you need it.

We have included some sample DOS documents on our website under Resources, so feel free to use them and tailor them to your experiences. Your DOS should be a reflection of you and your service, since it will be the official document that Peace Corps keeps on file and the document most employers will want as the summary of your service. Take your time, have fun with it, and don't put it off until the last minute!

Traveling

"*Traveling post-Peace Corps before returning to the States can be a great way to process your experience and slowly transition back to life in the U.S.,*" writes PCV Ben. "*After completing my service in St. Lucia in September of 2009, I backpacked with four other Volunteers through Central America. As leaving St. Lucia proved to be very difficult for all of us, despite the fact that many of us were looking forward to completing our services, it was great to be able to experience that process with other people who were in the same situation and were experiencing similar emotions. Additionally, in traveling through other developing countries where the culture was obviously different than St. Lucia but arguably more similar than St. Lucia to the U.S., we were able to slowly adjust to cultural differences, ultimately making adapting to life in the U.S. perhaps a bit easier.*"

Using the readjustment allowance for travel is a popular idea that many Peace Corps Volunteers actively pursue. Finally riding those motorcycles you couldn't touch during service or finally CouchSurfing at someone else's place for a change can be a welcome adventure. If you are interested in this option, finding other COSing Volunteers to travel with, like Ben did, can make it even more incredible.

"Never go on trips with anyone you do not love."
ERNEST HEMINGWAY

RPCV Travel Guides

Many PCVs and RPCVs talk about writing their own travel guides for their host countries ,and Other Places Publishing has really taken that idea and ran with it. As a small start-up publishing company founded by RPCV Christopher Beale (Antigua 05-07), it is dedicated to, *"Bringing the local knowledge of select countries to our readers. Our strength lies in utilizing Returned Peace Corps Volunteers who are intimately familiar with the local culture and possess an intuition for what independent travelers need and want."*

Their catalog of books is expanding rapidly, with almost 20 travel guides going into 2011 covering countries, including Ghana, Georgia, Benin, Madagascar, Namibia, Kyrgyzstan, Antigua and Barbuda, Dominica, Cape Verde, Thailand, Bulgaria, Tonga, Mongolia, and Micronesia and Palau.

"Our vision is simple," writes Chris: *"to have Returned Peace Corps Volunteers write travel guides about their country of service. We believe that RPCVs know their country of service better than anyone and possess invaluable information for travelers."*

Lead writers, in addition to gaining incredible experience in the literary world, get great commissions from every book. Many Volunteers turn these into scholarships in their host countries or find other ways of giving back. If you are interested in writing a travel guide for your host country or updating an already existing guide, visit www.OtherPlacesPublishing.com.

Bringing the World Home

Back before the invention of the internet, the Third Goal of Peace Corps—that charge to "promote a better understanding of other peoples on the part of Americans"—mostly happened once you were physically back on U.S. soil. Today, the Third Goal happens throughout your Peace Corps service—and maybe even before you swore in.

From the moment you updated your Facebook status to "OMG!!!

I'm going to Kyrgyzstan!!!!!" and all your friends commented back "Where the @#$% is that??" you've been educating your fellow Americans about a new and unknown part of the world. Volunteers today blog throughout their application process; they tweet that they've been sworn in; they post photos on Flickr and videos on YouTube.

What's more, you may have received visitors from home during your service. Believe it or not, there was a time when Peace Corps actively discouraged visitors during one's service. Oh, how the times can change. Perhaps Dad or Sis stayed with you at your site, had a mini-Peace Corps experience of their own, and returned home to tell all *their* friends about how amazing the Togolese people are, and the great work their daughter or brother is doing over there. This is the ripple effect.

But now, you're about to go back home. You might be asked to make a presentation at the local Rotary Club lunch, or to a Girl Scout troop for Thinking Day, or in a classroom as part of the annual Peace Corps Week (starting March 1st every year). Be prepared. In fact, here is a little list of things you might want to do to prepare for that eventuality:

> *"The wisdom of this idea is that someday we'll*
> *bring it home to America."*
> JOHN F. KENNEDY

Prepare to Bring the World Home

- Take lots of pictures before you COS—of people, the local market, your neighborhood, transportation you used…everyday things.
- Be sure to have good photos of yourself "in action" as a PCV!
- See above. Trust us there will come the day when you will need to have photos of yourself as a Peace Corps Volunteer. We're sure that Peace Corps Volunteer Aaron Williams

never imagined that someday he'd be Peace Corps Director Aaron Williams. Same goes for journalist Chris Matthews or astronaut Joseph Acaba. Have those photos ready for when you make it big.

- Keep a diary of some sort. Don't just write when things are going poorly or just when things are wonderful. Either way, you'll have a distorted record of your time overseas. Write regularly.
- Bring home indigenous clothing items. That may be all you are wearing right now and the idea may seem incredibly dorky. Regardless, it's great to have local dress for show and tell when you give a presentation or are marching in a presidential parade.
- Think kids. Chances are very good that in the future you will be asked to share your Peace Corps service with groups of kids. Bring home child-sized indigenous clothing items for both sexes. Kids have an absolute blast trying on clothes from other cultures. And someday, when you have kids of your own, they'll be the stars of International Night at their school. If you have room, an example of a locally made child's toy is a great conversation starter.
- Pack hard to find, unusual items that you most likely could never find in the U.S. For West Africa, it might be a small mortar and pestle and "charms." Elsewhere it might be a unique musical instrument, a game, or a ritual object.
- Bring home local music. It brings the memories.
- If you learned an obscure language, pack language instruction materials so you can keep up your language skills.
- Do *not* bring home an untapped ostrich egg. Just…don't.

Speaking Out

No one is banging on your door, asking to hear about your amazing time in Vanuatu? Be proactive. Sign up with the Speakers Match program, an NPCA and Peace Corps partnership.

Speakers Match connects former Volunteers with American classrooms in their local communities to talk about topics including public service, foreign cultures, language, and geography. Interested classroom teachers and Returned Peace Corps Volunteers can learn more and enroll in the Peace Corps' Speakers Match program by visiting www.peacecorps.gov/wws/speakersmatch/.

Also, as a Returned Peace Corps Volunteer—someone who has lived for two years at the grassroots in a foreign culture—you have a perspective, a worldview, which few others have. One powerful way to bring the world home, as well as to help you make sense of your Peace Corps experience, is to link your experiences in your host country to political and social action in the place where you study or live now.

NPCA is the longest-running advocate on behalf of the Peace Corps and its values, with long-standing, established relationships with congressional members and staffers. Together we are helping generate a set of innovative new ideas for a better and bolder Peace Corps, getting Peace Corps into countries it hasn't served in before, reinforcing "Third Goal" efforts, and scaling Peace Corps Volunteer initiatives. With more resources and relationships with Peace Corps member groups than any other organization of its kind, NPCA is leading the way in helping Returned Peace Corps Volunteers continue reaching out at home and abroad. To learn about this and more, visit www.peacecorpsconnect.org/advocacy.

You've Got 30 Seconds

"Another thing that takes some getting used to is feeling like people expect you to sum up your Peace Corps experience in 30 seconds or less," writes PCV Ben.

PCV Mike agrees: *"One of the most surprising things about coming home was how little people know or care about the Peace Corps...It's strange that we have this amazing experience traveling to the far corners of the world, doing amazing things with amazing people, and we come home and no one cares."*

"While it can seem like people just don't care about your experience abroad, which occasionally might be the case," continues Ben, *"I think that more so people who haven't served as a Volunteer or done something similar just don't understand how impactful and life-changing the experience is. Given that, sometimes it's difficult to feel understood. That's why I think it's important to keep in touch with fellow PCVs from your country that just ended their service, as well as to link up with an RPCV community, if possible."*

It won't be easy, but we hope resources like this handbook and people like your close friends and fellow Volunteers can help with the crazy process of readjustment.

In Peace Corps 101, our Peace Corps course which complements this book, Marisa recommends having a 30-second speech, a 3-minute speech, and a more in-depth speech in your mind when you talk with people. That way, you can feel out what the person you are talking to is ready for and meet them where they are.

Being and Doing

One of the most striking differences between America and many Peace Corps countries is the "worth through doing" culture that is so pervasive in the United States. PCV Ben shares the following story:

"After having served as a Volunteer in St. Lucia, where people are more focused on "being" and living day-to-day, the bombardment of 'what's next?' questions by people was a bit overwhelming. I told myself that coming back I would give myself a couple of months to relax, enjoy time with family and friends, the holidays, and my brother's wedding, but it became difficult to be completely at peace with this when I was asked daily what my plans were now that I was back. In retrospect, I think people were probably just trying to make conversation, but it definitely showed me how much we value what we do here in the States. I also observed that many people in the States seemed so busy and stressed out, not having time for friends or family, or themselves, and that turned me off. At the same time, I remembered being frustrated every now and again in St. Lucia with the fact that many people, in my estimation,

didn't "do" enough. There seemed to be a lot of talk, but little action or follow-through. So, I went from being frustrated with feeling like people didn't do enough while serving as a Volunteer to being frustrated with feeling like people were doing too much here in the States, thinking that everyone here just needed to take a major chill pill. I came to the realization, however, that I can't worry about what everyone else is or is not doing, but that I just have to work to create a sense of balance in my own life. Seven months later, working two part-time jobs and going to school part-time, I can tell you that it's not easy to resist getting sucked back into the 'go, go, go' mindset here in the States, even with a heightened awareness that this mentality exists. At the same time, even though I would consider myself to be a busy person, I do think I'm staying true to what I initially learned coming back."

Your Next Step

"I think one thing that is unique about Returned Volunteers is the urge to get back out there," writes PCV Mike. *"The Peace Corps doesn't quench that desire; if anything, it fuels it. After the cheeseburgers and beer stop tasting amazing and people stop asking where you have been for the past couple of years and you no longer appreciate every toilet you sit on for the technological marvel that it is, you start to look up and see airplanes flying overhead. You start to get that feeling that you should be hitting the road again, the euphoria of smelling another land. You look at your friends that you left behind and see that they are doing the exact same thing that they were doing when you left and realize that is the scariest thing that can happen to people like us."*

Whether it's through Peace Corps Response, keeping in touch with your friends back in your host country, joining up with NPCA and your favorite group of RPCVs, or helping us write the next edition of *The Peace Corps Volunteer's Handbook,* we hope you continue to follow that urge to get out there and change the world. Patient, flexible, and wise—becoming a Returned Peace Corps Volunteer really can just be your next step in changing the world.

MY NOTES

RESOURCES

T HE FOLLOWING INFORMATION HAS been helpful to many Volunteers over the years, but as we have said before, every Peace Corps experience is unique. Whether you are looking over the 27-Month Cycle or using information found on Peace Corps Wiki, please keep in mind that there is often no right answer in Peace Corps. Departure dates change, experiences vary from country to country, and expectations can often be far from reality.

Use the following resources as tools, helpful reminders, and sources of inspiration but please take each of them with a grain of salt. Take each experience as it comes, relax, and remember that most Peace Corps Volunteers come out the other side of their service having used their heart as much as their head.

The 27-Month Cycle

This was taken directly from *Critical Periods in the Life of a Peace Corps Volunteer*, written by Senegal PCVs many years ago. Please note that this list was made specifically with only the more challenging aspects of Peace Corps in mind. All Volunteers have wonderful experiences in Peace Corps, but they are generally consistent across all months and the creators of this list only included the challenges so that other Volunteers could see that those aspects of Peace Corps are shared amongst all Volunteer experiences around the world. Please write your own experiences down too so that we can create an "Unofficial 27-Month Cycle" for the next edition of *The Peace Corps Volunteer's Handbook*.

MONTH	ISSUES	BEHAVIOR/ REACTION
1	• Depart States • Disorientation • Health • Self-Consciousness	• Anxiety • Loneliness • Feeling Incompetent • Nervous about Personal Changes Over 2 Years
3	• Too Much Structure • Too Routine • Group Constancy • Fatigue • Impending Affectation • Language	• Withdrawal • Anxiety • Restlessness • Easy Irritation • Low Tolerance Level
3–6	• Assignment • Separation/Solitude • Uncertainty of Role	• Fright • Frustration with Self • Loneliness • Weight/Health Changes • Homesickness • Uselessness

INTERVENTIONS	YOUR EXPERIENCE
• Group Building/"Encounters" • Social Events • Establish Routines • Maintain Link Home • Develop Interests, Hobbies, and New Habits	
• Explore Independence • Visit City Areas • Make Plans for First 3 Months • Visit New Site • Establish Relationships & Familiarity with Peace Corps Staff • Gather Skills for Immediate Use	
• Develop In-Country Correspondence • Welcome Host Country Visitors • Visit Peers/Friends • Establish Support Links with NGOs • Technical Research for Future Use • Language Study • Establish Schedule, Routine, Create a Sense of "Home" • Hobbies To Do in Public • Simple Projects: Trees, Small Garden	

MONTH	ISSUES	BEHAVIOR/ REACTION
7–10	• Slow Work Progress • Language Plateaus • Cross Cultural Frustration/Shock	• Comparison to Others • Over-Zealousness • Homesickness • Uncertainties about Adaptation Abilities • Intolerance with Host Culture
11–15	• Mid-Service Crisis • Doubt of Program, Role, Self, Gov't • Reflection on Various Failures Over Time: Disillusionment, Confusion Resolving Frustrations & Victories • New Trainees Arrive • Holiday Time	• Impatience with Self and Program System • Blame on Program • Constant Complaining • Lethargy • Haughtiness with New Trainees via Super Identification with Image and Dress
16–20	• Increased/More Defined Work Pace • Project Work • Awareness of Time Constraints • Realization of One's Own Limitations • Consideration of "Post Peace Corps"	• Hyperactivity or Apathy • Procrastination • Self-Recrimination • Resignation • Disappointment • Downgrade Achievements • Over-Identification in Behavior

INTERVENTIONS	YOUR EXPERIENCE
• Reunions • Letters Home to Forgotten Relationships • Talk with Friends about Slow Starts & Failures • Simple Projects: Cooking, Personal Crafts, Meetings, Garden for Self • Consolidate Friendships • Use Language for Stories	
• Holiday Planning/Mini-Vacation • Review Work Plan • Set New Goals • Plan Vacation • One Year Anniversary Celebration • Develop New Recreation Options • Write Long Lost Acquaintances • Explore Better Relations w/NGOs • Return to Language Study/Practice	
• Visit/Assist New Volunteers • Physical Activity, "Get In Shape" • Focus on Relationships in the Town • Re-Examine Goals and Time Frame • Apply for GREs and Write Grad Schools • Explore Work Possibilities in Neighboring Towns	

MONTH	ISSUES	BEHAVIOR/ REACTION
20–23	• Prepare for Close of Service: Work and Follow Up • Depression about Perceived Lack of Accomplishments • Anticipated Separation • Demanding Work Pace • Consideration of Extension and Post Peace Corps Options • Acknowledged Chance of Unmet Goals	• Monument Building • Withdrawal into Work Details • Panic • Procrastination • Frustration with Self • Moodiness
23–27	• Trauma of Departure • Concerns about Social Re-Entry • Bridging Host Country Identity with Former United States Identity • Re-Definition of Career • Closer or Re-Definition of Host Country Relationships	• Fright • Confusion • Alienation • Anxiety • Panic • Giddiness • Impatience • Obsession with Planning and Scheduling

INTERVENTIONS	YOUR EXPERIENCE
• Vacation/Travel • Review Work Plans and Assess Feasibility • Plan "Closing Out" and Follow Up • Work with Counterparts, Gov't, Town Groups on Planning for Departure • Collaboration with 1st Year PCVs • Consider Post Peace Corps Planning • First Draft of Resume • 4-Month Personal Calendar • Give Quality Time to Colleagues and Personal Friendships	
• Check on Trends • U.S. Popular Culture Amongst Trainees • Do Self-Analysis: Factors of Self-Growth, Work Accomplishments, Consolidate Self-Confidence • Work on Self-Image • Shop for Art and Crafts • Write Friends • Make Social Plans • Post-Peace Corps Travel Plans • Transfer Work Skills and Area-Specific Knowledge to Trainees • Arrange for Gifts to Host Family	

Peace Corps Resources

Here are some of our favorite resources for Peace Corps Volunteers, bringing together information, people, and experiences. While all of these resources can be very helpful, please view each one carefully and objectively. Especially with personal opinion or wiki information, it is often up to the reader to determine quality and accuracy.

Great Peace Corps Resources Online

Peace Corps 101
(www.travishellstrom.com/peacecorps101)
An online course with dozens of Peace Corps Volunteers from
    around the world on how to make the most of your service.

National Peace Corps Association
(www.peacecorpsconnect.org)
Incredible information and interaction led by the National
    Peace Corps Association and tens of thousands of members
    worldwide.

RPCV Mentoring Program
(www.rpcvmentoring.org)
Joint program between Peace Corps and the NPCA to
    connect mentors with mentees and Peace Corps.

Peace Corps Facebook Group
(Search "Peace Corps" on Facebook)
Great place for discussions and finding other Volunteers.

Peace Corps Connect on Facebook
(www.facebook.com/peacecorpsconnect)
Place for PCVs, RPCVs, and future PCVs to get together on
    Facebook.

Live Your Purpose Coaching
(www.liveyourpurposecoaching.com)
Coaching resource by Sara Jones, mentioned in the RPCV
    section.

Quora on Peace Corps
(www.quora.com/topic/Peace-Corps)
Advice from people around the world on Peace Corps.

Literature

Insider's Guide to Peace Corps by Dillon Banjeree

A Few Minor Adjustments by Peace Corps

RPCV Handbook by Peace Corps

Helpful Organizations

88 Bikes Foundation
(www.88bikes.org)

Awesome Foundation
(www.awesomefoundation.org)

Engineers Without Borders
(www.ewb-usa.org)

Kiwanis International
(www.kiwanis.org)

Mercy Corps
(www.mercycorps.org)

Other Places Publishing
(www.otherplacespublishing.com)

Rotary International
(www.rotary.org)

Water Charity
(www.watercharity.com)

World Scouting Movement
(www.scouting.org)

World Vision
(www.worldvision.org)

Life Resources

More great resources mentioned throughout the handbook.

Optimal Living

ZenHabits
(www.ZenHabits.net)
A place for people who want to develop healthy habits and
simplify their lives.

PhilosophersNotes
(www.PhilosophersNotes.com)
CliffsNotes for Optimal Living Books with free scholarships
for Peace Corps Volunteers.

Couch Surfing
(www.CouchSurfing.org)
Free places to stay around the world.

10-Day Silent Meditation Retreat
(www.dhamma.org)
Vipassanna Retreats are a free, non-religious activity run by an
international non-profit that has served millions of people.

Effectiveness & Greatness

7 Habits of Highly Effective Teens by Sean Covey

7 Habits of Highly Effective People by Stephen Covey

The 8th Habit: From Effectiveness to Greatness by Stephen
Covey

PROCEEDS

A PORTION OF THE PROCEEDS from *The Peace Corps Volunteer's Handbook* go to fund Peace Corps projects around the world. We achieve this through the Peace Corps Partnership Program, which is connected with Volunteers on the ground making a difference in the lives of their community friends every day.

We are also researching other ways to use this funding to be more effective at helping Volunteers in their meaningful service every day. Peace Corps is an ever-changing organization and we will continue to grow as a resource to help Volunteers however we can.

We always hope to help achieve the three goals of the Peace Corps and fulfill the Peace Corps mission by assisting Volunteers to have happy, healthy, and meaningful service experiences.

By buying this handbook, you have already helped fund Peace Corps projects around the world and we'd love for you to get more involved!

The fun thing about a handbook is that it will always be a work in progress, becoming better and better by the hand of the person who is reading and adding to it. This is the beginning of a conversation about your Peace Corps experience and one small part of the worldwide Peace Corps community. We would love to hear your suggestions and contributions so that we can improve this resource with your help.

Please visit travishellstrom.com/handbook to share your comments, suggestions, and contributions with us any time. If you want to provide us with your information, we will be sure to thank you personally and include your name in our next edition.

Author Travis Hellstrom and his wife,
Tunga, in Peace Corps Mongolia
(2011).

ABOUT THE AUTHOR

AFTER GRADUATING FROM COLLEGE, Travis started his service as a Peace Corps Volunteer in eastern Mongolia in 2008. He worked in partnership with several agencies, including the Sukhbaatar Provincial Health Department, Provincial Hospital, Children's Center, State University, and Mercy Corps. In his third year, he served as a Peace Corps Volunteer Leader in the capital city of Ulaanbaatar, working at the Peace Corps Mongolia headquarters as well as the World Health Organization and the National Mongolian Scouting Association.

Following Peace Corps service, Travis has worked as a humanitarian consultant in Mongolia and throughout the United States. After his third year in Peace Corps, he stayed a fourth year in Mongolia co-founding the first TEDx event in Mongolia, serving as Founding CEO of New Media Foundation and helping certify the first B Corporation in Asia, The New Media Group. Travis graduated from SIT Graduate Institute as a Peace Corps Fellow and started his our company, Advance Humanity, which became one of the first dozen Certified B Corporations in Vermont.

Travis currently lives in Vermont with his wife Tunga, where he writes and continues to be one of the people crazy enough to think he can change the world. To learn more about Travis, visit www. TravisHellstrom.com.

Peace Corps 101

travishellstrom.com/peacecorps101

THE 6 WEEK COURSE

With Over 100 Volunteers, RPCVs
and Peace Corps Staff

THE CLASS

How to Change Your Life
with Peace Corps

INTERVIEWS

With Over A Dozen
Amazing Volunteers

Featured In